MONOGRAPH

THE ORIGIN OF THE BALTIC AND VEDIC LANGUAGES

Baltic Mythology

Interdisciplinary Treatise

Janis Paliepa

Dipl. Ing., B.A. (Hon. anthro.), M.Sc.

Ethnolinguist

authorHOUSE®

AuthorHouse™
1663 Liberty Drive
Bloomington, IN 47403
www.authorhouse.com
Phone: 1-800-839-8640

First published by AuthorHouse 4/7/2011

ISBN: 978-1-4567-2902-8 (sc)
ISBN: 978-1-4567-2901-1 (e)
ISBN: 978-1-4567-2900-4 (hc)

Library of Congress Control Number: 2011900823

Printed in the United States of America

Any people depicted in stock imagery provided by Thinkstock are models, and such images are being used for illustrative purposes only. Certain stock imagery © Thinkstock.

This book is printed on acid-free paper.

Tongue
    my mother's -
    the only one;
    trampled,
    nigh extinguished.
    As my only mother,
    thus her tongue –
    lest be honoured,
    lest forgotten.

TABLE OF CONTENTS

LIST OF MAPS, FIGURES, AND TABLES

Maps

Figures

FOREWORD

Once the study of myth and mythology acquired scientific recognition, anthropologists travelled to every corner of the world and visited every known cultural group, however small, to discover and establish the paradigm of universality to the human thought process.

At the same time, and almost in the geographical centre of Europe, lived the Baltic people, who belonged to an ancient culture but who essentially escaped the attention of historians and anthropologists. What could be the reasons for this oversight?

The small Baltic nations have endured the yoke of the German Empire, the Russian Czarist Empire, and the Soviet Union. These totalitarian and colonial powers were not interested in participating in any serious scientific inquiry that could awaken the self-esteem, the striving for freedom, and self-determination of these oppressed nations. In fact, the German and Russian empires practised ethnocide and genocide against the Baltic nations.[1a]

NOTE TO THE READER

This monograph, to my knowledge, represents the first attempt ever to carry out a comparative analysis of the Latvian mytho-poetic verses called 'Dainas' with the Vedic hymns of Rg-veda and Atharva-veda. The genesis of the Dainas remains unknown, and historians and linguists are not in agreement regarding their origin. For these reasons I researched scientific publications in various disciplines to determine the probable time and location of the origin of the Dainas. This research effort began at Concordia University in Montreal some 20 years ago, and formed the core of my Master's studies at the Université de Montréal. The research resulted in a comparative analysis of Latvian Dainas with Vedic hymns, and was published as a monograph *Latvju Dainas un Vedu Himnas* in the Latvian language in Riga, Latvia in 2004. (ISBN 9984-743-24-1)

Chapter 2 of the monograph is expanded to introduce the reader to Latvian nation, history, language, and mytho-poetics. This knowledge is essential to understanding the Latvian mytho-poetic Dainas, as the conclusion to this monograph postulates that the Baltic (Latvian and Lithuanian) languages are older than the Vedic Sanscrit language.

One challenge was how to establish an affinity between the quasi-forgotten mythological Latvian Dainas and the much translated and analysed Vedic hymns. Two non-Latvian scientists of the past intimated the direction to take and how to approach the mytho-poetic affinities. The German philosopher J.G. Herder (200 years ago) and the French linguist M. Jonval (80 years ago) described the Latvian Dainas as an archaic inheritance from the very beginnings of the Indo-European (I.E.) language community. This led to the conclusion that the origin of the affinity between the Latvian Dainas and the Vedic hymns is situated in the time period when various I.E. languages separated from the common cladistic language tree. Even though the existence of the Latvian Dainas and their archaic character was acknowledged some 200 years ago, and alluded to in recent scientific publications, no serious follow-up has been attempted by the international community of scientists. The reasons for this lack of interest are given in Chapter 2 of the monograph.

In this monograph anthropologist J.C. Lévi-Strauss' method of structural analysis is applied to uncover the hidden meanings encoded in the mytho-poetic Dainas. Conventional anthropological terms, such as 'oral history', 'folklore', 'religion', and 'mythology', are reviewed.

The monograph begins with an analysis of language developments during the dispersal and migrations of the I.E. peoples. Other scientific disciplines, such as geography, archaeology, and history, are also considered. With the help of the linguistic and mythological disciplines, the similarities and parallelism between the thematics in the Latvian Dainas and Vedic hymns are revealed. This, in turn, helped to determine the approximate time and location of separation of the Indo-Iranian and Proto-Baltic peoples and their languages.

The arrival of the first I.E. in 'Old Europe' coincided, in time and location, with the decline of matriarchy in the indigenous Danubian social structure. As a result of acculturation a new hybrid culture evolved. The Latvian Dainas reflect matrifocalism with the prominent functions of the mythical 'Mothers'-- the female deities – as well as the dominant role of women in the ancient Baltic social structure. Traces of the matriarchy of Old Europe have survived in some egalitarian form in modern Latvian daily life today. For these reasons a discussion of the role of Danubian culture is included in the monograph.

To summarize, an interdisciplinary monograph evolved to include a study of the migrations of I.E. people, along with the diffusion of their languages across the Euro-Asian continent. From the time of separation of the common Proto-Baltic and Indo-Iranian language, the Baltic people remained in close proximity to the geographical location of the separation. They retained the original common I.E. language and thus maintained its archaic character. These languages are still spoken in Latvia and Lithuania today, and together with the Indo-Iranian language, they lead back to the same archaic time period. In other words, it is conceivable that the living Baltic languages are older than the dead Vedic Sanscrit language and represent the oldest existing Indo-European languages.

Author 2011

CHAPTER 1: GENERAL INTRODUCTION

The Objectives of the Monograph

The last 20 years have seen a resurgence in the research of the languages and cultures of the I.E. peoples. The Baltic and Vedic languages, which are particularly archaic, have played an important role in these studies.

The research presented in this monograph deals primarily with the question of the similarities and the parallelism found in the Latvian mytho-poetic Dainas and the Vedic hymns. As an extension of the main theme, two supportive themes, the 'Danubian matriarchy' and a 'New hypothesis' of I.E. migration, are added to broaden the scope of the monograph.

The Latvian Dainas and the Vedic hymns were chosen because their mytho-poetic material has a common archaic origin. The parallels between the cosmologies of these two mytho-poetic corpuses are striking and are also supported by a series of linguistically related key words.

It is presumed that this parallelism and the similarities are inherited from a common past of the two branches of the Indo-European language family: the Indo-Iranian and the Proto-Baltic. These two linguistic sources are chosen for two reasons:

First, both linguistic branches are extremely archaic: the Vedas represent one of the oldest documented Indo-European languages; the Dainas – as well as the Baltic languages and cultures in general – have also been acknowledged for their archaism by linguists.

Second, the two mytho-poetic corpuses are globally comparable. In both cases they originated in pastoro–agricultural societies with comparable economic routines. Since the central theme of the monograph deals with the cosmic circulation of rain/water, the economic parallels are relevant.

In addition, the author is of Latvian origin and with my first language being Latvian, I have direct access to one of the texts of the two mytho-poetic corpuses treated in the monograph.

An important fact to emphasize is that the language and the mythology of the hymns of the Rg-veda and Atharva-veda have been extensively researched and published. This is not the case with the mytho-poetic Latvian Dainas. It was only some 200 years ago that an internationally known non-Latvian, the German philosopher J.G. Herder, in his publication *Stimmen der Voelker in Liedern,* characterized the Latvian Dainas as follows:

> *"Latvian folk-poetry represented the (Latvian Nation's) archives of the past, their science, mental alertness, and the records of ancient events".*

A number of scientists have recognized that the Baltic languages contain extremely archaic linguistic elements. This could be attributed to the fact that the Baltic nations have lived relatively isolated from external influences over some 4000 years. Therefore, the Balts have retained certain cultural and linguistic elements, including mode of thought and traditions that can be traced back to the common origin of the Indo-Europeans. It can also be presumed that the Latvians of today are jointly the guardians as well as the creators of their mytho-poesy.

The Vedic hymns and Latvian Dainas contain an aspect of cosmology that supports the main theme of the monograph. The relevant cosmology is represented by the atmospheric movements of rain/water – the vital fluid for human life – between the sky and the earth. For these reasons, the Dainas that contain references to the deities of water, rain, wind, storm, and the earth are compared to the celestial and terrestrial deities described in the Vedic hymns and devoted to the Maruts (celestial deities) and Mother Earth (deity of earth). The monograph does not present an inventory of all the celestial and terrestrial deities found in the two mytho-poetic corpuses. It explores the parallelism and the similarities of certain thematic topics.

The Organization of the Monograph

The principal theme of the monograph is an attempt to show that a common approach is possible between the themes of the Latvian Dainas and the corresponding themes of the Vedic hymns.

Considering the fact that readers may not be familiar with the Latvians and their mytho-poesy, Chapter 2 is entirely devoted to an introduction to the Latvians, their language, and their mytho-poetic Dainas.

The Vedic mytho-poetic material is briefly presented in Chapter 3. The analysis and the comparison of the Dainas with the Vedic hymns in relation to the role of the deities of water, wind, and storm are presented in Chapter 4. The supportive themes, the Danubian matriarchy and the migration of the Indo-Iranian peoples (the New hypothesis) are covered in Chapter 5. A general review and discussion of the themes follow in Chapter 6. The conclusions of the results of the comparative analysis of the verses of the two mytho-poetic sources and the supportive themes are summarized at the end of Chapter 6. An appendix suggesting a probable transposition of names and words from the Baltic (Latvian/Lithuanian) languages to the Vedic Sanscrit completes the monograph.

Definitions and Presuppositions

The meanings of conventional terms and phrases continually change over the passage of time. These changes are particularly visible in the abstract terms that belong to the higher levels of human cognition. Some of the most frequently used terms in the monograph are reviewed and redefined to avoid ambiguous interpretation as their meanings may have changed or have remained frozen in time. It is recognized that terminology is culture dependent and as such reflects the attitudes of society in its evolution. Ruth Finnegan reminds us of the typical attitude towards the oral tradition within social anthropology:

> *"The study of verbal arts and oral traditions has long seemed a Cinderella subject within British social anthropology, in the past often treated as more a matter of folklorists, oral historians or linguists rather than mainstream anthropology,.......Some answers are probably empirical and culture dependent. The relation between variation and stability in texts, together with how this is conceived of and practiced, may vary between cultures, genres, historical periods, even individuals".*(Finnegan: 163).

These remarks support the fact that the conventional terminology of the past ought to be reviewed. Since the theme of the monograph is based on the study of mythological material whose origin is found in the oral tradition, the terminology is prone to ambiguity and contentiousness. For these reasons an effort is made to elucidate the meanings of the relevant terms.

Oral and Written History

Anthropology is known as the 'Science of Man', but it could also be called the 'History of Man' — all that people have thought and done from the past to present. Thus the sciences of anthropology and history are inseparable. However, in the past the mainstay of history was exclusively based on written sources, leaving the rest to prehistory. On this subject Indian anthropologist S.C. Malik writes:

> *"Prehistory is commonly regarded, if not often, as something very remote and mysterious and which, at the most, may be considered useful for mere chronicling purposes".* (Malik: 11).

Consequently, oral history was quasi-forgotten and reduced to taciturnity. The mytho-poetic material that was researched almost exclusively comes from societies and people 'without history' (in the conventional meaning of the term 'history'). However, oral history has gradually taken its proper place among the other disciplines of cultural anthropology. Written history has been with us for only some 4000 years, whereas oral history goes back to the beginnings of human speech.

The Reliability of the Historio-linguistic Texts

The research of a subject from a specific historical era can only be supported by the facts and theories available at that time. When new facts become known, usually as a discovery, older published materials continue to disseminate obsolete, even false information.

During the 19th century, the dominant hypothesis among European, in particular the German, linguists and historians postulated that the I.E. people migrated from India to Europe. However, the discovery at the beginning of the 20th century of the ruins of two great ancient cities (Harappa and Mohenjo-Daro) of the Indus Valley civilization reversed this hypothesis. These cities did not have the I.E. cultural character, and had existed and flourished well before the arrival of the I.E. people.

The Indo-Iranians, a branch of the Indo-Europeans have, in fact, entered the Indus Valley coming from the West. The dominant hypothesis was reversed but the libraries still hold volumes based on an obsolete concept.

The case of the culture of Harappa is presented as it has serious impact on the studies of the migration and languages of the I.E. people and their historio-linguistic evolution. Did the Indo-Iranians penetrate the Indus Valley coming from the European region – the ancient Danubian culture area – or did they arrive via another itinerary? These questions are reviewed in Chapter 5.

Folklore

The term 'folklore' was first used to describe, generally, the traditions of the peasantry, but eventually was also applied to other activities of a society. Thus the term has become ambivalent and very vague.

Denoting also the oral tradition, the term 'folklore' appeared in the scientific literature some 300 years ago. It designated all traditions of the ordinary people as compared to those of the elite – the aristocracy and clergy. The socio-economic structure (feudal) in Europe created a visible difference between the cultural activities of the elite and those of the lower class – the artisans and peasantry. The term folklore acquired an inferior status with socially discriminatory nuances. For these reasons the usage of the term 'folklore' is avoided when analysing the cultures of diverse ancient societies.

Religion and Mythology

The conventional linguistic meanings of the terms 'myth' and 'religion' are nebulous and their usage in anthropological studies could be very wrongly interpreted and even disputed. This observation applies particularly to the term 'religion', which appeared in the European languages with the expansion of Christianity. The term was probably borrowed from the Latin `res-ligio' or `res-ligo', which signifies all that people have in common and keep them together. In Latvian the term religion was introduced only in the 17th century, and is not found in the ancient language of the Dainas.

For generations the disciplines of cultural anthropology, such as folklore, ethnology, and mythology, have been penetrated by religious elements. Anthropology overemphasized religious content while seeking religious expression in various cultures through their rituals, songs, dances, visual arts, and ceremonial activities. The theologian J. Campbell found it necessary to denounce the idea that a homology could exist between religion and mythology. He defined myth and religion as:

> `From the point of view of any orthodoxy, myth might be defined simply as 'other people's religion', to which an equivalent definition of religion would be 'misunderstood mythology', the misunderstanding consisting in the interpretation of mythic metaphors as references to hard fact".* (Campbell: 55)

Here Campbell criticizes the conventional meanings of the terms 'myth' and 'religion', and also the fact that the institutionalized church has degraded the scientific meaning of myth to raise its own prestige and importance. Moreover, J.C. Lévi-Strauss also has written:

> *".........l'anthropologie semble être progressivement détachée de l'étude des faits religieux. Des amateurs de provenances diverses en ont profité pour envahir le domaine de l'ethnologie religieuse".*[1] (Levi-Strauss 1 :235)

To compare texts originating from various sources it is necessary to clarify the terms 'to believe' and 'God', terms that are always associated with a given culture (culture dependent).

To believe:

Religion is inseparable from the human mental ability to believe. The terms 'to believe' and 'religious convictions' are tied to absolute verities and as such they play an important role in the studies of comparative mythologies. The terms 'to believe' and 'to believe blindly in something' do not exist in the language of Latvian Dainas. Instead, the Dainas contain the respective equivalents in expressions such as to be wise, to understand, and to be morally strong.

God:

'God', and the derivations of the term, such as 'goddess', 'demi-god', 'deity', 'divinity', and the divine mothers are used according to the conventional meanings. The signification of the term 'God', at the time of I.E. arrival in Europe, is unknown. As a term it has survived in most European languages. However, with the arrival of Christianity in Europe, its interpretation has acquired many nuances. Since the contents in this monograph refer to the time well before the era of Judeo-Christianity and Islam, the exact meaning of the term 'God' is not essential.

The meaning of Dievs (engl. 'God') in the Latvian Dainas is explained in Chapter 2, and for the Vedic hymns in Chapter 4.

The Method of Comparative Analysis

The mythological material used for the comparative analysis is presented by:

12 examples of the Latvian Dainas and
14 examples of the Vedic hymns.

These examples are all associated with the movements of rain/water from the celestial vault to the Mother Earth. The celestial and terrestrial deities of the Dainas are presented, and the movement of rain/water is graphically shown in a model; the Vedic gods are briefly described and also shown in a similar model.

The methodology used was inspired by the postulates of Lévi-Strauss, especially by his writings in *La structure des mythes*, where he states:

> ``*Nous posons, en effet, que les véritables unités constitutives du mythe ne sont pas les relations isolées, mais des paquets de relations, et que c'est seulement sous forme de combinaisons de telles paquets que les unités constitutives acquièrent une fonction signifiante*''. [2] (Levi-Strauss 1 : 242)

Lévi-Strauss' assertion is verified by the structure and the contents of the Latvian mytho-poetic quatrains, the Dainas. Read directly, the structure of the Dainas is easily recognized as an assemblage of the constitutive units that semantically represent the contents (substance), which are wrapped by tropes and symbolism. Additionally, Lévi-Strauss postulated that myth represents a particular form of language and that mythical relations could be understood in binary terms. The structural model for a mytho-poetic quatrain is established by treating it as a myth in miniature that is structured by packets of relations based on binary oppositions. By unfolding the syntagmatic text to a paradigmatic level of relations, the emergence of the cosmological backdrop becomes visible. The parallelism of the cosmological aspect of the mytho-poetic verses is remarkably similar between the Dainas and Vedic hymns, which is also supported by the comparative thematic analysis in Chapter 4.

The structural model is presented in Table 1 below. Three examples of representative Dainas are chosen: A – represents the cosmogonic/cosmological type, B – represents the moral code, and C –the stimulus of independent thought.

Table 1

Latvian	English
Daina A: cosmogonic/cosmologic	
33773-54 No jūriņas izpeldēja- Dieva dēlu kumeliņi; Vienam bija zvaigžņu sega, Otram saules apausīši.	From the sea came swimming- Colts of the sons of Dievs; One with a cover of stars, The other with a mane of sun.
Daina B: moral code	
33199 Ej, bāliņ taisnu ceļu- Runā taisnu valodiņu; Tad i Dievs palīdzēs, Taisnu ceļu nostaigāt.	Follow, dear brother, an honest path- Speak an honest language; Then Dievs will help you, To walk an honest path.
Daina C: stimulation to think	
33679, var. Kur, Dieviņi, tu paliksi-	Where, dear Dievs, will you sojourn-

Kad mēs visi nomirsim	After we all will die;
Ne tev tēva, ne māmiņas,	You have neither father, nor dear mother,
Ne tev savu bāleliņu.	Nor your own dear brothers.

Daina A (cosmogonic/cosmologic)

Source:	Invocation:	Symbolic:	Empiric:
Anonymous creators <u>Motif:</u> Inscribe in the subconscious the stimulus to learn about the universe	Help by the supernatural: <u>The sons of Dievs</u>	Colts of the celestial sea, <u>the cover of stars the mane of sun</u>	The sky <u>The night sky</u> <u>The day sky</u>

Daina B (moral code)

Source:	Invocation:	Symbolic:	Empiric:
Anonymous creators <u>Motif:</u> Inscribe in subconscious the stimulus to lead an honest life	Help by the supernatural: <u>Dievs</u>	<u>Honest path Honest language</u> (path = life)	Purpose <u>to lead an honest life</u>

Daina C (stimulation to think)

Source:	Invocation:	Symbolic:	Empiric:
Anonymous creators <u>Motif:</u> inscribe in subconscious the stimulus to think	Question to the supernatural: <u>dear Dievs</u> (dim. 'Dieviņi')	Future of Dievs tied to <u>human life</u>	Encourage <u>independent thought</u> about the world and life

In these examples we find the constitutive units assembled to form a mytheme - a myth in miniature. These contain the collective motivation (in the mythic era), the imagined supernatural medium, the symbolic means of expression, and their effect on life in the real world. In each Daina three steps of transformation are discernible to arrive at the empiric educative result: Daina A teaches how to understand the universe and daily celestial events - the night and the day, Daina B encourages one to lead a moral and ethical life, and Daina C stimulates thought about life and creation. The clear and simple language of these Dainas confirms two theories of Lévi-Strauss:

1. Mythical thought is as rigorous as the scientific and is comparable to it.
2. Structural analysis can be applied to mytho-poetic verses in general and to the quatrains of Latvian Dainas in particular.

Binary oppositions are employed to uncover the multiple meanings of the individual Dainas, which very often contain allegorical expressions. The multivalent symbolism is easily recognizable in the following example:

3005

Latvian   **English**

1. Mana balta māmuliņa-   1. My dear mother is all white-
2. Mani baltu darināja(audzināja); 2. White she raised (nurtured) me;
3. Apvilkusi baltu kreklu,   3. Clothing me in a white shirt,
4. Pacēlusi saulītē.   4. She lifted me in the dear sun.

Var. 3025

3. Pati māte dubļus brida,   3. She herself walked a muddy path
4. Mani nesa rociņā.   4. Carrying me in her arms.

It can be easily seen how this Daina, together with the variant of the two last lines (3 and 4), reveal the symbolism fully wrapped in the quatrain. Here 'white' (Latvian 'balta') is simultaneously and symbolically presented as the color, the dress, being radiant, the loving, and one with moral principles. Possibly, the dominant symbol refers to a moral principle, and the symbolic meaning is expressed by a simile. It is also possible that the symbolic significance of 'mother' with 'white' hair is expressed by a synecdoche (one for a whole). The role of the sun is expressed in a diminutive and affective form 'saulīte' (from 'saule' in Latvian, 'sun' in English). The meaning of line 4, 'She lifted me in the dear sun', is associated with the very best a mother can endeavour for her child. This group of quatrains has numerous variants where we can find many linguistic and poetic expressions that show how the ancient Latvians organized the verses in a variety of binary oppositions: white – black (color), white – black (clothing), white (radiant) – black (sombrous), white (tenderness) – black (coldness), white (morally strong) – black (immoral), white (clean) – black (dirty).

Lévi-Strauss' theories and postulates, as they are applied to the lyrical material, are summarized and discussed at the end of Chapter 2, in the subsection, *Lévi-Strauss and the Latvian mytho-poetics*.

CHAPTER 2: THE LATVIANS, THEIR LANGUAGE, AND THE DAINAS

Introduction

The Recollections of Ancient Historians-Travellers

For the last 700 years, except for a short period of 20 years after World War I, the Latvians belonged to one of the 'forgotten peoples' of European history. Therefore, it is important to establish their existence as one of the Baltic peoples, with their own language, culture, and folk poesy called 'Dainas'. The commentaries found in the writings of ancient historians-travellers are presented.

The first to mention the Balts is the Greek historian Herodotus (Rawlinson: 235) of the 5th century BC. He wrote of a people called 'Neuri', who inhabited the lands north of the 'Scythian farmers' living along the coast of the Black Sea. Most historians have accepted the hypothesis that the Neuri could be considered as belonging to, or forming a part of, the ancient Balto-Slavic people. A more accurate description is provided by Roman traveler and historian Tacitus, who in the year 98 AD, after criss-crossing the German lands, became historically the first to encounter the ancient Baltic people whom he named 'Aiisti'. In his writings we find this description:

> *"Turning, therefore, to the right hand shore of the Suebian[3] sea, we find it washing the country of Aiisti, who have the same customs and fashions as the Suebi, but a language more like the British. They worship the Mother of the gods, and wear, as an emblem of this cult, the device of a wild boar, which stands them instead of armour for human protection and gives the worshipper a sense of security even among his enemies. They seldom use weapons of iron, but clubs very often .They cultivate grain and other crops with a perseverance unusual among the indolent Germans.... .They*

are the only people who collect amber – "glaesum" their own word for it – in the shallows or even on the beach. Like true barbarians, they have never asked or discovered what it is or how it is produced. For a long time, indeed, it lay unheeded like any other refuse of the sea, until Roman luxury made its reputation." (Tacitus: 139)

Some historians have suggested that the name Aiisti is semantically closer to the Estonian people. However, the fact that Tacitus writes about the Aiisti as the gatherers of amber, and no amber is found on Estonia's coast, the remarks made by Tacitus about the Aiisti most likely are attributable to the Westernmost Baltic tribes – the Prussians.

The name Balts originated later, and today it is popularly applied to the three largest nations: the Prussians, the Lithuanians, and the Latvians. Together, they all belong to the I.E. language family called the Baltic. The inhabitants of the modern-day Baltic nation of Estonia linguistically belong to the Finno-Ugric language group.

The Balts and Their Languages

During the Bronze age and up to the 9th century, an immense territory of Eastern Europe was inhabited by the Baltic-speaking people. After the expansion of the eastern Slavs (predecessors of the Russian nation), from the 5th to the 10th century AD, this territory was greatly reduced to the southern and western shore region of the Baltic sea. The Latvian tribes occupied the north-east, the Lithuanians the center, and the Prussians the south-west of the north-east territory of the European continent (Map 1). Their existence, their lands, and their cultural characteristics are described in scientific publications. Other Baltic nations, such as the Jatvingians and the Galindians, have not survived.

Map 1
(Gimbutas 1: 63)

The Bronze and the Early Iron Age of the Maritime Balts

Maximum extent of the Baltic culture during the Bronze Age

The grey territory covers the land mass inhabited by the ancient Balts. The blackened (by author) territory shows the reduced area after the expansion of the Eastern Slavs.

The common links between the Baltic peoples were their genetic parentage and their language. As a language family, they are shown on the cladistic language family 'tree' of the I.E. languages, presented graphically in Figure 1. The new tree was developed by the linguists of the University of Pennsylvania in Philadelphia, with the help of mathematicians and the most powerful computers. According to these linguists, the new cladistic language tree is more accurate than the language trees developed in the past.

The archaic character of the Baltic languages is best described by J. P. Mallory:

> *"The texts, as indeed the modern Lithuanian language today, has always attracted the attention of linguists since, despite their recent date, they appear remarkably archaic in terms of Indo-European linguistics. To take a familiar example, the Lithuanian proverb 'God gave teeth; God will give bread' displays an almost incredible similarity to its translation into the much older Latin and Sanscrit:*
> *Lithuan.: Dievas dave dantis, Dievas duos duonos*
> *Sanscrit: Devas adadat datas, Devas dat dhanas*
> *Latin: Deus dedit dentes, Deus dabit panem*
> *Latvian: Dievs dod zobus, Dievs dos maizi (anc. dona);(line added by the author)*
> *Because of this transparent conservatism, many linguists hold that the Baltic languages, like their Slavic neighbours, have probably moved but little since late Indo-European times."* (Mallory: 82)

The Latvian language shows the same 'incredible similarities' with Latin and Sanscrit.

Figure 1

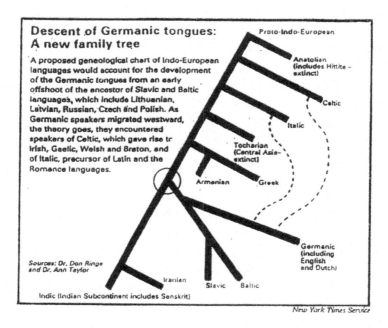

The new cladistic tree of the Indo-European languages. <u>Note</u>: the circled juncture (added by the author) shows the point of separation between the Proto-Indo-Iranians and the Proto-Balts.

A member of the linguistic family of the Baltic languages, the Prussian language died out about the 17th century; the Latvian and Lithuanian languages are still spoken in Latvia and Lithuania today.

The arrival of the Crusaders of Sword Brothers (a branch of the Templars) from Central Europe is considered to be the most tragic event in the history of the Baltic peoples. After a brutal 100 years of incessant wars with the Latvian tribes, they were defeated and dispersed, and the Crusaders appropriated their lands. The Germanic and Russian expansion continued under the patronage of the two Christian Empires, the Holy Roman Empire from the West and the Byzantine from the East.[5] The territory of the two surviving nations, the Latvians and Lithuanians, was further reduced during the following centuries as shown on Map 2.

The Lithuanians retained their political power until the 16th century. The Prussian tribes, after the uprisings of 1260-1272, were crushed by the Teutonic Order. In spite of Prussian resistance in the defense of their land and freedom, they could not match the well-armed European Crusaders. The Crusaders followed the German Emperor with the support of Roman Curia under Pope Gregory X, who issued a Bull proclaming a holy war against the Prussians.[6] After the 17th century the Prussians ceased to exist as a nation and as a cultural entity. The Prussian language continues to survive only in a few dictionaries as compiled by German priests and, together with the archaeological finds, are witnesses to the ancient lineage with the Baltic culture.[7] The fate of the Prussians represents an unrecorded genocide in the history of Europe.

Map 2
(Gimbutas : 23)

Fig. 1. Baltic tribes and provinces c. A.D. 1200

The reduced territory of Latvia and Lithuania since 1991; (the thickly dotted borders are drawn by the author). The Prussians were absorbed by the Germans from the 13th to 17th centuries. The latvian tribes: Lettigallians, Selonians, Semigallians, Curonians.

The Recovering and Publication of the Dainas

At the cultural horizon of the Baltic peoples the most significant representatives are the Latvian and Lithuanian mytho-poetic verses called the 'Dainas'. The Latvian Dainas were collected during the 19th century and published at the beginning of 20th century. More than 182,000 primary verses, together with their variants, constituting a total of 1,250,000 verses, were collected over 50 years. The first volume of Dainas was published in 1894.

Kr. Barons (1835-1923), a Latvian intellectual, is considered to be the principal initiator of the coordination, collection, classification, and transcription of the entire corpus of the Latvian Dainas, published under the title *Latwju Dainas*. Kr. Barons accomplished his life`s ambition and all the collected verses were published in six volumes by 1915. In 1970-1980 prof. Vaira Vīķis-Freibergs of the Université de Montréal, jointly with her husband, prof. Imants Freibergs of the Université du Québec à Montréal, transcribed the complete corpus of Dainas on to the computer. This project is known as the *Boston-Montreal Database of Latvian Folksongs,* based on the Copenhagen edition. The complete corpus of the original edition (Kr. Barons) of *Latwju Dainas* is now available on the Internet. The importance of these mytho-poetic Dainas, in the field of cultural anthropology, is best desribed by prof. Albert Lord of Harvard University :

> *"Krišjānis Baron's contribution to Latvian cultural development by recording its distinctive past cannot be overestimated.....He also made possible, through his collecting and publishing of Latvian traditional song, the study of that immense, and very often very beautiful, poetic corpus so that it might add the Latvian evidence to the problems of oral traditional poetry in general. It is one of the largest, perhaps indeed the largest, body of oral traditional lyric poetry songs in existence."*[8]

Another non-Latvian, Michel Jonval, a graduate from the l'École Normale Supérieure (Paris, France), and lecturer at the University of

Latvia, was engaged in the research of comparative mythologies; he wrote:

> *"Ces chansons (les Dainas), dont nous n`avons que quelques restes et qui ont traversé des siècles de servitude en gardant cette pureté d`expression et cette noble allure, évoquent une mythologie qui, en son épanouissement, aurait peut-être pu rivaliser d`éclat et de poésie avec les plus belles mythologies des peuples indo-européens".*[9]

It is important to note that the mythological Dainas possess a universal character, since they, generally, do not make any reference to peoples, nations, or races. They do not even refer to Latvians as such, who are either their creators or, perhaps, just their caretakers.

The Survival of the Dainas

The traditional folkloric material of the Latvians (including the Dainas), which was dormant for centuries, was finally revealed some 200 years ago. Several non-Latvians helped to resurrect this cultural material, and have made it accessible to linguists and historians. The most well known of these early collectors and publishers is the German philosopher Johann G. Herder. He was born in Mohrungen, East Prussia, and worked as a teacher at the Domschule (Episcopal School) in Riga, Latvia, from 1764 to 1769. Herder, who lived in a multicultural environment, observed the problems that exist in a sratified society: the oppressed Latvian peasantry, the German landowners and nobility, and the Russian Tsarist administration. In his writings Herder described the case of small nations, degraded economically and culturally, and dominated by more powerful nations, who are invariably ethnocentric and prejudiced.[10]

J.G. Herder returned to Germany where, after his death in 1807, his anthology titled *Stimmen der Voelker in Liedern* (The Voices of Peoples in Songs) was published. Among the songs of diverse nations are also 79 Latvian Dainas in the Latvian language, translated into German. Two of these Dainas of the mythological/cosmogonic type, handwritten by Herder himself (translated into English by the author), are presented:

Johann G. HERDER
Born 1744 in Mohrungen
East Prussia
Died 1803 in Weimar, Germany
Herder Institute, Marburg, Germany

Song
The Daughter of Sun boasted
To throw the sea on the hill,
With mittens of silk,
And with a pitchfork of gold.
The Sons of Dievs followed her
Looking for her wreath;
The Sun polished small chalices
Standing in the middle of the sky.

These two Dainas, selected by Herder, are not yet fully deciphered nor understood.

The first serious effort to resurrect the Dainas belongs to the pastor G. von Bergman, who collected 490 folkloric songs, and in 1807 published them under the title of *Erste Sammlung Lettische Sinngedichte in Livonia'* (The First Collection of Latvian Mindsongs in Livonia - North Latvia). In East Latvia, the Latvian ethnologist J. Sprogis transcribed and translated 1857 folkloric songs into Russian and published them in Vilna, Russia (now Lithuania) in 1868, titled *Pamjatniki Latisskogo Narodnago Tworcestva* (Collection of Latvian Folksongs). The most significant effort was accomplished by pastor Bielenstein who in 1874 published 4793 folksongs.[11]

The Contribution of Kr. Barons

Krišjānis Barons at his desk amid
the sent-in manuscripts
Member of the University of Latvia
Born: 1835 in Strutele, Latvia
Died: 1923 in Riga, Latvia
Photo: from A. Arājs
book *Kr.Barons un
Latvju Dainas*, p. 221,
Riga, Zinātne, 1985

The collection of Dainas and other folkloric material, such as fables, legends, proverbs, and riddles, was accelerated at the end of the 19th Century. Under the direction of Kr. Barons, the Dainas were transcribed and published by 1915. The publication was financed by the Latvian businessman H. Wissendorff in collaboration with the Imperial Russian Academy of Sciences in Petrograd, Russia. A corpus of 1,250,000 verses of Latvian folk-poetry was published in seven volumes under the title *Latwju Dainas* (Latvian Dainas). A reproduction of the cover of the first volume is shown in Figure 2.

Kr. Barons classified the Dainas according to the human life-cycle, from birth to death with its celebrations, such as nuptials, marriages, and funerals, and also the traditional festivities surrounding the solstices and equinoxes. Kr. Barons adopted the fundamental principle of not arbitrarily correcting the verses, and transcribed it just as it was received orally from the semi-literate Latvian peasantry, mostly women.

The collection of folkloric material continued after 1915, particularly during the years 1918-1940, when Latvia was an independent republic. However, this material is not considered here because the more recent the folkloric material, the less it contains mythological significance. A number of other publications of Dainas, covering different subjects have been published during the 20th century by Latvian ethnologists and linguists. Among them, the artist and army officer Ernests Brastiņš initiated an original approach to the Dainas, and together with other Latvian artists and intellectuals, they laid the foundations for the Latvian ethnic religion based on the ideology contained in the Dainas. His most notable publications were *Cerokslis* (Catechism) in 1932, *Dieva dziesmas* (Songs of God), and *Latviešu tikumu dziesmas* (Latvian Virtues in Songs) in 1928.[12]

Unfortunately, the Dainas have not attracted the attention of cultural anthropologists, mythologists, historians, or linguists. The reasons for such indifference are discussed in the following pages.

Figure 2

Reproduction of the cover of the first volume of Latwju Dainas, printed and published in Jelgava, Latvia, 1894

The Contribution of Michel Jonval

During the years of scientific indifference, the selection and publication of 1219 mythological Dainas in 1929, by French linguist Michel Jonval, can be regarded as an exception. M. Jonval lectured at the University of Latvia for a number of years and during that period acquired the Latvian language and also an extensive knowledge of Latvian folklore. He writes that his interest in Latvian folk poetry was encouraged by the recommendation of Antoine Meillet, his student, a renowned authority of I.E. languages.(Jonval:7)

In the introduction of his book, 'Les Chansons Mythologiques Lettonnes' (Latvian Mythological Songs), M. Jonval draws attention to the subject of authenticity concerning all folkloric material. He noted that if there is any doubt about the authenticity of a very ancient oral tradition, or if there was a tendency to embellish certain details of that mythology, it can, nonetheless, be assumed that the original signification is not lost. The fact that the oral tradition becomes known to us in fragments, is proof that these fragments pertain mostly to an archaic character. M. Jonval also noted that in the Dainas, *"....there is always an extremely important pre-Christian nucleus in which, besides the pure Latvian concepts, such as the role of the Laima (deity of fate), we clearly distinguish the other deities such as Saule (the Sun), the daughters of Saule, the sons of Dievs, as being inherited from the Indo-European epoch".* (Jonval: 5).

M. Jonval elaborates further that:

> *"La mythologie lettonne nous est connue par quelques données fragmentaires et tendancieuses contenues dans les chroniques de prêtres allemands venus combattre le paganisme, et par les traditions populaires, proverbes, contes et chansons. Ce sont surtout les chansons, les Daïnas, qui, transmises oralement de génération en génération jusqu'à nos jours, nous offrent des matériaux d'une extrême richesse sur la vie et les croyances des anciens Lettons".*[13]

M. Jonval published a volume of 1219 Dainas chosen for their mythological and religious character, which were extracted from the corpus of Dainas published by Kr. Barons. These Dainas were published in the Latvian language with translations in French and classified as follows:

> 120 verses describing Dievs
> 340 verses describing the deities of the sky
> 270 verses describing the deities of the earth
> 405 verses describing the deity Laima
> 84 verses describing the deity of the dead

This selection, as published by M. Jonval corresponds fully with the originals from the corpus of Dainas by Kr. Barons. For the comparative analysis with the Vedic hymns a selection of the mythological Dainas are taken from those collected by M. Jonval. The Dainas devoted to the deity 'Māra', are an exeption as they were not included in the Dainas published by M. Jonval. These are taken directly from the Kr. Barons corpus. Māra is a personification of the deity 'Zemes Māte' (Mother Earth). Her functions are compared with those of the 'Great Goddess', which are discussed in Chapter 5 under the heading *The Matriarchy and the Vital Fluid*.

Dainas: Ethnographic Selection

Before the analysis of individual Dainas, and to familiarize the reader with their mytho-poetic style and metaphorical genre of expression, an ethnographic selection is presented. These examples numbered 1 to 20 are organized in five major categories and reflect the cultural traits of the ancient Latvians. Note: the Dainas used for the comparative analysis in Chapter 4 are identified according to the numeration of Kr.Barons, eg, 34067.

These five categories of Dainas reflect the following:

1. Cosmogony and cosmology
2. Life and nature
3. The moral code
4. Beauty and aesthetics
5. Social and political life after the arrival of the Crusaders and Christianity

All Dainas are conceived in two rigid metrical rhythms – trochee octosyllabic (80%) and dactyl hexasyllabic (20%) – and orally transmitted in the form of a poetic quatrain. The first two lines (1 and 2) consist of a question or a statement; the last two lines (3 and 4) either provide an answer or amplify the motif or contents of the first two lines. The following is an example of the type trochee octosyllabic:

Latvian	English
1. Ģērbies, Saule, sudrabā-	Dress Sun in silver-
2. Nu nāk tavi vedējiņi;	Your guides are coming;
3. Ūdens zirgi, akmens rati,	Horses of water, chariots of stone,
4. Sudrabiņa kamaniņas.	A sleigh of silver.

This cosmogonic type of Daina was chosen as an example for its structure as an octosyllabic trochee and for its metaphorical expression. It contains four lines of eight syllables, each divided into four metrical units, with the first syllable always accented. Literally read, it does not make much sense and it is not yet fully deciphered nor understood. It possibly conceals a situation or event in nature (sky) and is formulated as a metaphorical quatrain. Or, it may be a mythological and cosmogonical metaphoric expression describing the preparations for the marriage of Saule (deity of the Sun).

Most Dainas are self-explanatory, and only those Dainas that contain philosophical and mythological elements are further commented.

1. The Cosmogonical and Cosmological Dainas

Latvian	English
1.	
Kur Dieviņi, tu paliksi-	Where, dear God, will you sojourn-
Kad mēs visi nomirsim;	After we all die;
Ne Tev tēva, ne māmiņas,	You have no father, nor dear mother,
Ne tev savu bāleliņu.	Nor your own dear brothers.

This Daina poses a philosophical question. Of note is that 'Dieviņš' here represents the diminutive and affective form of Dievs (God) who is treated as a member of a family. The question, however, could convey a deeper signification. If we all die, what will happen to Dievs? The most probable answer would be that if a society (people) perishes, their Dievs will perish with them. (The nature of Dievs in the Dainas is described in Chapter 4.)

2.

Dieviņš jāja rudzu lauku-	Dear Dievs rode across the rye field-
Ar akmeņa kumeliņu;	With a colt of stone;
Pelēks bija rudzu lauks,	Grey was the rye field,
Pelēks Dieva kumeliņš.	Grey the colt of Dievs.

3.

Māte, mana mīļa māte-	Mother, my dear mother-
Ne tu mana mūža māte;	You are not my eternal mother;
Tā Saulīte, tā Zemīte-	It's the dear Sun, it's the Earth-
Tā ir mana mūža māte.	They are my eternal mothers.

Daina 3 is also one of a philosophic nature. The totality of human life is presented as consisting of two existences: the corporal life received from one's mother and the other life associated with that of Saulīte (the Sun) and with that of Zemīte (the Earth). Saulīte and Zemīte represent the diminutive and affective forms of Saule (the Sun) and Zeme (the Earth). The Daina is self-explanatory; the totality of human life, whatever it is, is tied to the life of the sun and earth.

4.

Pērkons brauca pār jūriņu-	Pērkons rode over the sea-
Lietiņš lija jūriņā;	The rain fell into the sea;
Arājs lūdza Pērkonīti-	Arājs prayed to dear Pērkons-
Brauc, Pērkoni šai zemē.	Ride Pērkons to this land.
Brauc, Pērkoni šai zemē-	Ride Pērkons to this land-
Miežiem asni novītuši.	The barley sprouts have wilted.

Here Pērkons represents the deity of thunder; 'arājs' (pron. 'arāys') represents someone who works the land.

2. Dainas Devoted to Life and Nature

5.

Mīļās Māras istabiņa-	The small room of dear Māra-
Pilna sīku šūpulīšu;	Is filled with tiny cradles

Kad to vienu kustināja-	If one of them is moved-
Visi līdzi šūpojās.	All will sway together.

6.

Lēni, lēni bērziņš auga-	Slowly, slowly grew the small birch-
Lēni lapas darināja;	Slowly it developed leaves;
Lēni augu pie māmiņas-	Slowly, I grew by my mother-
Gudru ņēmu padomiņu.	Wisely I partook her advice.

7.

Ēdiet, govis, zaļu zāli-	Cows, eat the green grass-
Neminieti kājiņāmi;	Do not crush it with your feet;
Gauži raud zaļa zāle-	Sadly cries the green grass-
Kājiņāmi samīdama.	Crushed by your feet.

8.

Zīlīte, žubīte-	''Zīlīte'', ''žubīte''-
Tās manas māsiņas;	They are my sisters;
Tās skaisti dziedāja	Beautifully they sing
Upītes malā.	Beside the small stream.

Daina 8 is conceived as an hexasyllabic dactyl, the six syllables in each line are divided into two dactyllic strophes. 'Zīlīte' and 'žubīte' are the names of two small songbirds found in Latvia.

3. Dainas Devoted to the Moral Code

The songs in this group are assigned to social and moral behavior.

9.

Ej, bāliņ, taisnu ceļu-	Follow, dear brother, an honest path-
Runā taisnu valodiņu;	Speak an honest language;
Tad i Dievs palīdzēs-	Then also Dievs will help you-
Taisnu ceļu nostaigāt.	To walk an honest path.

This Daina was analyzed, as an example, in the *General Introduction*.

10.

Caur sidraba birzi gāju-	I walked a grove of silver birches-
Ne zariņu nenolauzu;	Not a tiny branch did I break;
Būt zariņu nolauzusi-	If I had broken a tiny branch-
Tad staigātu raudādama.	Then I would have walked crying.

Daina 10 warns a young girl: if you walk through a grove of silver birch trees (a morally pure life), do not break even a tiny branch. If you break one, then you will continue walking through life in tears.

11.

Kādi bija tie ļautiņi -	What kind of people were they-
Kuri otru nicināja;	Who loathed others;
Vai bij Dieva labumiņa,	Were they of Dievs goodness,
Vai Saulītes baltumiņa.	Or the whiteness of dear Saule.

12.

Audz, mana pādīte -	Grow, my dear infant-
Audz, labi tikusi;	Grow up with honour;
Tikušu vajaga-	We need the honorable-
Šai saulītē.	In this dear sun.

4. Dainas Devoted to Loveliness and Aesthetics
13.

Daiļa mana rota bija -	Beautiful was my bijou -
Smuidrs mans augumiņš;	Slender my body;
Rotu pati darināju -	The bijou I made myself-
Laima smuidru augumiņu.	Laima my slender body.

14.

Brāļu māsa sētiņā -	The sister in her brothers' yard -
Kā saulīte istabā;	Is like the dear sun in a room;
Nebij zelta, ne sudraba -	With neither gold nor silver-
Tik baltās villainītes.	With only the white shawls.

15.

Dziedādama es uzkāpu -	Singing I walked up -
Baltābola kalniņā;	The hill of white clover;
Lai krīt mana grezna dziesma -	May my graceful song fall-
Baltābola ziediņā.	Into the flower of the white clover.

16.

Skrej, bitīte tai zemē -	Run, tiny bee to that land-
Kur mīt mana māmuliņa;	Where my mother sojourns;
Aiznes viņai mīļus vārdus -	Bring her loving words –
Zem spārniņa pasituse.	Under your tiny wings.

5. Dainas Reflecting the Social and Political Situation

17.

Dieviņš gāja tīrumā'i-	Dear Dievs went into the field –
Ar sidraba sētuvīti;	With a silver basket;
Kungam gāja smilgas sēti-	For the lord he sowed thistles -
Arājam'i miežus rudzus.	For the 'arājs' - the barley and rye.

18.

Ar varīti jūs kundziņi -	You, lords, have your power-
Ar padomu bāleliņi;	Brothers, your wisdom;
Ar varīti nevarēja -	With power one cannot -
Padomiņu pievarēt.	Prevail over wisdom.

19.

Uzvaltieši, nekrišņoni –	'Uzvaltians', you non-Christians -
Mūsu Dievam neticēja;	In our Dievs, they believed not;
Kluci sētā pakāruši -	By hanging a piece of wood-
Saka mūsu Pestītājs.	They say, that's our Saviour.

20.

Melnmēteli, melnmēteli -	Black robe, black robe –
Ko tu man elli soli?	Why promise hell for me?
Ne tev bija pierē ragu -	You have no horns on your brow-
Ne tev astes pakaļā.	Nor a tail in your behind.

Dainas 19 and 20 demonstrate the attitude of Latvian peasantry towards the clergy dominated by German priests: the piece of wood symbolizes the cross of Christ. Sarcasm is also visible in Daina 2o. In Daina 17'Arājs signifies an honorific term,representing the keeper of the land. 'Uzvaltians' are the people from a near-by village.

The Mytho-poetic Language of the Dainas

Any language acts as a mediator of a symbolic process between ideas and emotions, and the sounds emanating from the oral canal. Similarly, the language of Latvian mytho-poetry (Dainas) represents a symbolic process that acts as a mediator between the sounds of a natural language and the nuances of mythic significations. The Indian linguist Sunit Chatterji observed that the substantive Dainas possess a genealogic relationship with the words and roots of the Indo-Iranian and Avestan languages:

*"The Baltic word **'Daina'** had unquestionably its Aryan (Indo-Iranian) equivalent, etymologically and semantically which is perfectly permissible. It is strange how most of the authorities on Indo-European linguistics and culture have ignored this affiliation of the Baltic word **Daina** (Lithuanian **dainà**, Latvian **Daina**) to the Vedic **dhēnā** and the Avestan **daēnā**. ...Indo-European root *dhi, *dhy-ei, *dhei, meaning 'to think, to ponder over, to give thought to', appears to be the source of the Vedic **dhēnā** and Avestan **daēnā**. An Indo-European form *dhainā as the source-word can very easily and quite correctly be postulated. .....and (in) modern Vedic schoralship, it can only mean, according to the context, 'speech', 'voice', 'words', 'praise', 'songs of prayer', 'prayer', 'songs'".*(Chatterji: 69-73)*

S. G. Oliphant in the *Journal of American Oriental Society* (1912) concluded that:

*"**Dhēnā** is the exact phonetic equivalent to the Avestan **'daēnā'** and the Lithuanian 'dainà'. The 'daēnā' of the Avesta is (1) religion, especialy the Ahuran religion, also (2) a theological philosophical concept of the totality of the psychic and religious properties of man. It is the spiritual ego, the immortal part of man, the mental logos. The Lithuanian **dainà** is a folksong, but these folksongs contain the best and highest expressions of the native heart and mind. They are frequently the media of expressing their religious sentiments and their philosophical reflection".*

American critic, Robert Payne (in his Foreword to A. Greimas 'The Green Linden', *Selected Lithuanian Folksongs*) writes:

*"They (the Lithuanian **dainàs**) represent a form of poetry as ancient as anything on the earth, for they are essentially spells, incantations, offerings to the gods. Though they are simple and immediately comprehensible, they do not belong*

*to the world we know.......These poems to the gods show
no fear, nor do they plead for mercy".*

Along with the quote by Herder earlier, these three citations explain
the significance of the word Daina, as well as the underlying sense of
the Dainas. How do we explain the fact that the Dainas contain the
'mental vigilance' (Herder) and the word Daina signifies 'the mental
logos' (Oliphant), and that an equivalence is found within the Indo-
Iranian language family? As a response, it points to the relative archaism
of Dainas, as well as to the ideology of Indo-Europeans still contained
in the living Baltic languages, the Latvian and Lithuanian.

Myth and Dainas

Many linguists and historians are not fully aware that the Baltic
languages contain more Sanscrit words and roots than any other
European language. The affinity with the Sanscrit can be found in
the contemporary Latvian language, particularly in the mytho-poetic
quatrains – the Dainas. This affinity of the Lithuanian and Latvian
languages with the Sanscrit and Latin was well demonstrated previously
by J.P. Mallory. Generally, the ideology and cultural elements that
have arrived via the oral tradition have remained in the background,
together with their mythological components. The following table
shows the correlation of the term 'myth' and 'Daina' with the cognates
in Vedic/Avestan, Latin, Latvian and English languages. This presents
an overview of the roots of the key words as they are later used in the
monograph. The table also shows the semantic affiliations between the
terms as well as a number of various abstract meanings that are hidden
in these terms.

MYTH

Latvian	English	Latin	PIE*, Sanscrit, Avestan (ave.)
Mīt-s (a)	myth	mythus	mithas

Affiliations			
mute	mouth	mutus	*munthaz
māṇi sa-maṇa, at-miṇa,pie-mīt	mystery consciousness	mysterium conscientia	mani *mon-, men-
DAINA			
Daina			dhēnā, *dhaina daēnā (ave.)
Affiliations			
Diev-s (a)	God	De(us)	deva, dyaus *devah dēva (ave)
Diena, degt doma dot, deva	day, burning thought donate, don	dies côgitatiô donum	*dhegh *dhi-, *dhei- *dō-, *da-

The word 'myth' has changed its meaning over the centuries. Initially, the word 'mythos' in Greek described any utterance coming from the mouth(Gr.'muthos',Engl. 'mouth ', Latv. 'mute'). The conventional usage of the word 'myth' signifies a fabulous story, transmitted orally, which expounds symbolically the forces of nature and the human condition. According to J. P. Vernant:

> *"For the philosophical studies of the myth, the mythologue ought to associate the analysis of the contents to discover the semantic relationships, the interplay, the symbolic correspondences, the multiple levels of significations which enters the text, the hierarchy of the codes which are used in the message".* And by quoting Nilssen on the subject of ancient Greece, J.P. Vernant expands that myth is *".....a free fantasy in which the contemporary creations have described the popular beliefs, the superstitions of the peasantry which was still very close to the earth, where*

the sources of all religions and the great Gods evolved".
(Vernant: 208, 224)

The Interpretation and Translation of the Dainas

The interpretation of the Dainas, especially the cosmogonic ones, presents enormous obstacles if one tries to unravel and understand the symbolic significations. They are presented in lyrical mytho-poetic verses and wrapped in metaphoric expressions. Other difficulties lie in the fact that many Dainas have been corrupted during the centuries of forced acculturation by foreign occupants of the Baltic lands. The Dainas were labeled as the work of the devil by overzealous German priests and thus were driven into hiding.

It is important to mention that the Balts survived as the last 'pagans' in Christianized Europe for some six centuries. Baltic chiefs accepted Christianity for political reasons to avoid the never-ending wars with the aggressors, Crusaders from Central Europe. The submission and acceptance of Christianity by Baltic leaders did not filter down to the ordinary Baltic people (the peasantry), who continued to follow their ancient traditions and beliefs until about the 18th century. After this period the language of the Dainas commenced to deteriorate in daily usage to the point where Latvians themselves no longer understood their subtle and sublime meanings. Translating the Dainas became difficult because of the symbolism hidden in their abstract expressions. These difficulties are well defined by professor V. Vikis-Freibergs:

> *"If the Dainas have not received the international recognition which they so richly deserve as the largest single repository of published oral folklore, it is for the double reason of their belonging largely to a lyrical genre of poetry and the difficultes inherent in translating such material into other languages. In lyrical poetry.....form and content are so inextricably bound together that the medium is indeed the message, and to tamper with the medium in translation is neccessarily to impoverish the message"*.
> (Vīķis-Freibergs 1: 6)

Furthermore, the translations should also reflect the aesthetics and the beauty of expressions in a given language, together with the mythical significations. It is also important to try to associate oneself with the thoughts of the anonymous authors (of the Dainas) with an 'emic' insight (from the translator's perspective) in order to understand the message.

Translation from Latvian to English presents some specific difficulties. The Latvian language is inflective without articles and few prepositions. Therefore, English translations are longer and the loss of the metric rhythm becomes unavoidable. The structure of the Dainas is often allegoric and the affective and diminutive forms are frequently used. The metrics, the rigid trochees and dactyls cannot be restored, and any attempt to do so result in deficient and amateurish translations.

Lévi-Strauss and Latvian Mytho-Poetics

Lévi-Strauss' method of structural analysis has already been applied previously to the three examples of Dainas in the *General Introduction*. Here, the application of the theories of Lévi-Strauss to the analysis of Latvian mytho-poetic verses in general is discussed.In his writings on structural analysis, Lévi-Strauss primarily examines the narrative type of myths, whereas the Latvian Dainas represent lyrical mytho-poetic verses. However, Lévi-Srauss also emphasizes that the value of myth does not depend on the style, nor the syntax, and not even on the modes of expression. Therefore, the lyrical verses of the ancient Latvians are well suited for structural analysis by following the theories and postulates proposed by Lévi-Strauss. He assigned a permanent structure to myth, which is also singularly related to the past, present, and future. With the affirmation that the language and significance of the myth is found at a high cognitive level, it is also attested by the symbolic expressions, style, and language of the ancient Latvian Dainas. Lévi-Strauss applied his theories to both orally transmitted and written narratives that could be easily transformed. Such myths are subjected to the emotions of the storyteller or the writer, which could lead to diverse interpretations of the disguised symbolic meanings. During the process of transfer, the integrity and the original significations of the myth may also be embellished and distorted. The question is whether the mytho-poetic verses conceived in an inflective language can also be analysed the same way as mythic narratives? This applies, particularly, to the lyrical quatrains that were quantitatively reduced, simplified, and transcribed into the corpus of Dainas. There are a number of reasons by which these quatrains (mythemes) acquired their aesthetic qualities and intellectual values, and because of their universal nature, maintained their intrinsic structure and symbolism. For some 4000 years the Baltic people have inhabited a territory distant from the itineraries of intercontinental trading routes and were not significantly affected by the invading Asian hordes. The substantial reduction of their territory during the last 1500 years would suggest that they led a relatively peaceful existence and were not inclined to conquer the lands of their neighbours. As agrarians their mode of living was closely tied to nature and to the work in the fields. For these reasons their traditions and belief systems changed very little. During the long winter evenings they recited poetic verses, tales, proverbs, riddles, and songs. These traditions were transferred orally from generation to generation. Gradually, the poetic verses and songs were reduced to quatrains, then improved, polished, and structured in rigid syllabic meters, thus assuring their survival. The rigid meters, trochees, and dactyls protected these verses from corruption over the millennia. The Dainas that were created in the vernacular Latvian during the centuries after the arrival of the Crusaders and missionaries in the 13th century are of lower quality and as such easily recognizable.

The theories of Lévi-Strauss contain also elements of other sciences, such as linguistics, psychology, and biology. He has analysed human thought processes and proposed a universal approach to the development of diverse human cultures. He did not show much interest in the meanings assigned to the ideas and even the languages of people, but was more interested in their internal underlying structures, which he recommended to be studied, updated, and re-examined. Lévi-Strauss viewed the existence of the world as a continuum, and considered the underlying structures of our words and codified messages of information to be programmed in the human brain. Any of these programs would be partially either inherited or acquired during one's lifetime. For these reasons, diverse cultures, conditioned within different environments, perceive reality differently. Lévi-Strauss also concluded that the analogical and not logical cognition process is the general mode of human thought and represents the linguistic expressions in binary oppositions. Humans see and classify all phenomena in binary pairs, and cannot understand these and classify them if they do not have an opposite. A model of Time and History, based on the concepts of Lévi-Strauss, is presented below.

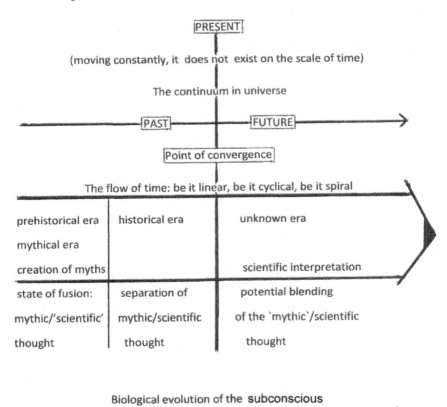

To complete the model, a citation by Lévi-Strauss is appropriate:

> *"Mais la valeur intrinsèque attribuée au mythe provient de ce que les événements, censées se dérouler à un moment du temps, forment aussi une structure permanente. Celle-ci se rapporte simultanément au passé, au présent et au future".* [14]

To summarize, the analysis of the lyric Dainas follows the postulates formulated by Lévi-Strauss:

1. Binary opposites can be applied as a mode of expression.
2. The mythical thought process is comparable to and equals the scientific.
3. Structural analysis can be applied to the mytho-poetic material in general.

The ancient Dainas respond well to these postulates, even if a Daina, separately taken, does not represent a phenomenon the same way as a conventional narrative (epopee, tale, etc.). Each Daina can be considered as one great constitutive unit – a single mytheme. As prof. V. Vikis-Freibergs states:

> *"The four line strophe is the atom of the Daina tradition*
> *in its smallest semantically and poetically integrated unit.*
> *Cast in a metrical mold of mathematically rigorous double*
> *symmetry, constructed according to an intricate geometry*
> *of parallels and contrasts, each quatrain, taken separately,*
> *is a self-contained epigram or a poem in a miniature'.*
> (Vīķis-Freibergs: 1: 8)

Thus the totality of the poem (quatrain) is sufficient to maintain its autonomy. However, only the 'superstructure' of the quatrain is thus represented, with the structure being the contents of the quatrain itself preserved in a logical order.

The most important phase of research is directed towards the deciphering of the significations that are 'imprisoned' in the microcosm of the quatrains, taking into account the fact that they express the thoughts of anonymous creators who lived in a prehistoric environment. To facilitate the effort of deciphering these mytho-poetic quatrains, the theories of Lévi-Strauss on the analogical thought process of the human mind and the application of the principle of binary oppositions are essential.

A feature applicable to the Dainas is that the binary oppositions are usually complementary rather than conflictive. In the ancient Dainas there is no distinction between those that are 'mythological' (containing the names of cosmogonic beings) and those without the 'mythological' content. The ancient Latvians lived in an environment where everyday life was intertwined with nature and cosmogonic concepts. There was no separation between the natural and cultural, between the sacred and profane. When interpreting and deciphering the mythological material, it is necessary to compare a large number of Dainas and their variants with similar thematics and motifs.

CHAPTER 3: THE VEDAS

The Vedas – An Overwiew

Whereas the Latvian mytho-poetic Dainas have remained almost unknown to historians and linguists, the Vedas have been studied in detail and published in hundreds of volumes. Therefore, the Vedas will be given only a short introduction.

The Vedic texts can be classified in chronological order as follows: Vedas (Veda Samhitas), Bramaṇas, Araṇyakas, Upanishads, and Sūtras. The Vedic mythology is vast and complicated, with hundreds of deities and thousands of divine entities. Because of their relative archaism, hymns from the Rg-veda and Atharva-veda were chosen for the comparative analysis with the Latvian Dainas. Hymns were selected that reflect similar themes and motifs as in the Latvian Dainas. Therefore, the hymns devoted to the deity Marut from the Rg-veda and those devoted to the deity Earth from the Atharva-veda were used. These hymns contain the thematic mythological elements that are associated with the movement of rain/water from the celestial vault to the earth. The Vedic texts have been transmitted orally over the millennia, by sophisticated mnemotechnics, before being written down some 300-400 years ago. According to J.P. Mallory:

> *"These were initially preserved only in oral form.......The earliest representative of this Old Indic is to be found in the Vedas, the ancient religious literature in India. The language of the Vedas is very archaic, and the cultural and geographical world portrayed in these hymns suggests that they were composed in northwest India before the first millennium B.C., with a notional date of around 1500-1200 B.C." (Mallory: 36,37)*

And according to Pierre-Sylvain Filliozat (1992, p.18):

"*Une seul chose est certaine, c'est la réussite de la transmission oral de textes védiques sur plus de quatre millénaires, même avant l'apparition de l'écriture qui n'est pas chose très ancienne en Inde. On observe que de nos jours où le secours de l'écriture est disponible, il existe les récitants capables de s'en passer totalement.*"[15]

The Vedic Mythology

The present situation of the Vedic mythology is very well described by Jamison and Witzel:

"*Indeed, what is striking about the Vedic pantheon is the lack of overarching organization. Some gods are transparently natural - their names merely common nouns, with little or no characterization or action beyond their 'natural' appearance and behaviour (e.g., Vata, deified Wind). Others are deified abstractions, again with little character beyond the nouns that name them (e.g., Bhaga Portion). Others belong especially to the ethical and conceptual sphere (e.g., Varuna, Mitra), others to ritual practice (Soma, the deified libation). Despite their disparate affiliations, the deities do not remain compartmentalized; gods of apparently different origins are often invoked together and can participate together in mythic activity. Whatever the history and sources of this complex pantheon, it cannot be reduced to a single organizational principle, nor can certain members, that might not conform to such a principle, be defined as outsiders and latecomers, given that gods of various types have counterparts outside the Vedic. It is well to remember Kuiper's structural(ist) statement (1962-1983, p.43) on the fundamental difficulty of understanding a single mythological figure isolated from the context of the mythological system*". (*Jamison-Witzel: 53*)

For the reasons mentioned above no inventory of Vedic gods is presented as the majority of them have been invented by poets of various fictive origins and backgrounds.

In general, the anonymous poets of the Rg-veda have conceived various cosmogonic schemes. They addressed their gods as the most glorious and powerful and, by exaggerating their accomplishments, the poets expected, in return, to receive compensation. In addition, the poets of the Rg-veda and Atharva-veda have included in their hymns some of the orally transmitted ancient ideas of the Indo-Europeans and described natural phenomena as sacred acts.

Vedic Ideology and Rituals (two examples)

Reciprocity

The Vedic phrase: 'dehi me, dadāmi te' (Yajur Veda 5.3.) closely resembles the Latvian: 'dod man, dodu tev'. Both phrases contain the principle of reciprocity between the actions of men and the gods. It signifies the cycle of perpetual exchange, as well as a code for the actual exchange of various substances, including the rites of oblation. These exchanges can take place between men and between the gods and men; just as the poet, by glorifying the gods, expects a generous return. The principle of reciprocity signifies also the perpetual exchange that takes place between the productive earth (the deity Earth) and the sky (the celestial gods). Likewise, the Vedic concept of reciprocity can also be characterized as a natural economy. The fruits of the earth (both plant and animal) are offered to the celestial gods, and in return, they deliver to the earth the vital fluid – rain/water. The cycle of reciprocal exchange between the earth and the sky represents also the cyclical order of cosmic harmony.

Vedic '*rta'

Another fundamental Vedic concept is contained in the word (root) *rta. In general, *rta expounds the 'truth' (respect for the truth) as well as the active realization of truth as a vital force between the actions of men and gods. The *rta is also associated with the cyclical order in life as well as with the cosmic movements. These notions – cyclical order and cosmic movements – are well reflected in the Latvian language.

<u>Cyclical order:</u> Latvian: 'dzīves **rit-s**', gen. '**rit-a**',

English: 'the **rythm** of life'.

<u>Cosmic movements:</u> Latvian: saule '**rit**' (infin '**rit.– ēt**') kalnā, lejā.

English: the sun is rolling up and down the hill.

In K. Karulis *Latvian Etymological Dictionary* (Karulis II: 125) two roots are discernible: ide. ***ret(h)** (same as in Pokorny) and the Vedic ***rta**. Most of the expressions associated with cyclical order and cosmic movements are derived from these roots.

CHAPTER 4: THE CIRCULATION
OF THE VITAL FLUID

Introduction

The comparative analysis of orally transmitted mythological texts, such as those of the I.E. languages, is well defined by Calvert Watkins:

> *"Comparative Indo-European poetics may be defined as a linguistic approach, both diachronic (genetic) and synchronic (typological), to the form and function of poetic language and archaic literature in a variety of ancient Indo-European societies from India to Ireland."* (Watkins: 270)

The analysis in the monograph is based on thematic concepts, mental images, and diverse forms of expression (tropes, symbolism). Taking into account that the mytho-poetic texts used in the comparison belong to higher levels of cognition, a figurative (mostly metaphoric) approach to their interpretation is applied. These texts cannot be interpreted literally because such an approach could not convey a comprehensive result and, in a poetic environment, could render them unintelligible. Therefore, the texts are translated 'sense to sense' and not 'word to word'.

The comparative analysis proceeds through three stages. First, mytho-poetic material is selected from the Dainas and the Vedic hymns that represent the circulation of rain/water between the sky and the earth. Second, it is shown that a cosmologic homology exists between these two pastoro-agricultural societies with polytheistic religions. Third, in a comparative linguistic analysis that includes grammatical elements (morphology and syntax), the diverse forms of expression and diachronic language changes are considered. A series of key words that are frequently found in the texts about the circulation of rain/water and are cognats within the Baltic and Vedic languages are also presented.

For example, by commencing with one keyword or a combination of keywords that represent a poetic image with an associated concept, the meaning of the entire verse or a phrase is determined. As an introduction, some of the keywords used later in the text are presented below. In Latvian two cases are shown: the nominative 'Dievs' and genitive 'Dieva'.

English	Latvian	PIE*
God	Diev – s (a)	*dei-
sky	debes – s (s)	*ak - mon
stone	akmen – s (s)	*ak - men
cloud	mākon – s (s)	*māk -
water	ūden – s (s)	*aued -
rain	lietu – s (s)	*lēi -
wind	vēy – š (a)	*vē -
tempest	vētr – a (as)	*uētra

For keywords the *IndoGermanisches Etymologisches Woerterbuch* by J. Pokorny is used; the meanings of the most significant (stone, water, and tempest) are given below:

Sanscrit: <u>Akmo-/-a,</u> Pok. I, p. 19, <u>asman</u> (old Indic), Pok, II, p.14: germ. Stein, Himmel, Steingewoelbe (latv. akmens, debess, akmens velve; engl. stone, sky, stone vault). <u>Udan,</u> Pok. II, p. 78, <u>udan, oued,</u> p. 42: germ. fliessen, Brunnen (latv. plūst (ūdens), aka; engl. flowing (water), well).

<u>Vrtra, vtra,</u> Pok. I, p. 83, <u>* uetra, uer -,</u> *<u>aue-diro,</u> (latv. vētra, aura; engl. tempest); vrtra, Pok. I, p. 1161, and II, p. 45: germ. Sturm, Gewitter (latv. vētra, vētra ar pērkonu un zibeni; engl. storm, storm with thunder and lightning.

The Latvian Poetic Material

Dainas: The Deities of Rain, Water, Wind, and Storm

The Dainas are identified according to the enumeration adopted in the original volumes of *Latwju Dainas* by Kr. Barons. The cosmogonic/cosmologic, celestial, and terrestrial deities, along with the multitude of divine mothers are schematically represented in Figure 3. The interpretation of their role is based on the Daina texts. The deities of the Dainas that are closely associated with the circulation of rain/water are briefly presented below, followed by a more detailed description of their activities.

DIEVS (God) is understood as a symbol of everything beyond human comprehension – **the supernatural.** A creation myth, in the conventional sense, cannot be found in the Dainas. Dievs did not create the universe and does not possess an omnipotent nature. Dievs sojourns in the sky as well as on earth among people, by participating in their daily activities.

SAULE (sun) in the Dainas is described as a celestial body, the cosmogonic companion of the Earth. As a deity, Saule is often mentioned as a protector of orphans as well as of the poor and the unfortunate. The cosmological Saule, as the source of light and heat, together with mother Earth, are providers of food and thus sustain all life on the earth.

PĒRKONS (thunder) and the sons of Pērkons represent also a duality: first, as a cosmogonic deity, he is admired and dreaded; second, as an entity observable in nature, he represents a powerful and destructive force. However, Pērkons, as the provider of the rain/water, is also venerated and welcomed.

ŪSIŅŠ (deity of horses) is represented as a guardian of horses as well as a provider of rain/water.

MĒNESS (moon) is the least popular celestial body, and is potrayed as the celestial voyageur, nocturnal and solitary.

MĀRA (Mother Earth) as a deity, symbolises all material entity (substance) on earth. Māra is responsible for the nutritive subsistence on earth, including human life – from the cradle to the tomb. Her functions extend, after corporal death, also to existence beneath the earth by maintaining the 'Veļi' community under the name of **Mira Māra,** the mother of Veļi. In the Dainas Velis (sing. of Veļi) represents the astral body (doublet) of humans that after death continues an existence 'as long as the sun remains in the sky' (Daina). In her activities on the earth, Māra is assisted by many 'Mothers', such as the Mothers of the wind, of the forest, of the sea, of the water, etc.

An example:

1872,v.2. Latvian
Mīļās Māras istabiņa-
Pilna sīku šūpulīšu;
Kad to vienu kustināja-
Visi līdzi šūpojās.

English
Dear Māra's small room-
Is full with tiny cradles;
When one is moved-
All sway along.

This Daina clearly shows the importance of the relationship and interdependence between all living beings on the earth.

LAIMA is a deity symbolising human fate. From the moment of birth Laima together with the deity Māra are the companions of every individual during his/her entire life.

Latvian
Ej, Laimiņa, tu papriekšu -
Es tavās pēdiņās;
Nelaid mani to celiņu,
Kur aizgāja ļauni ļaudis.

English
Go, dear Laima, before me –
I will follow in your footsteps;
Do not let me go that path,
Where the evil folk trod.

Figure 3

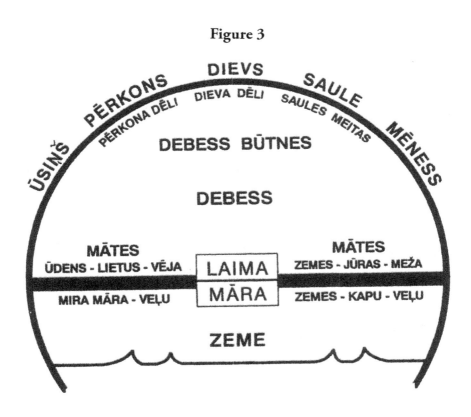

The celestial and terrestial beings are represented in the model above. These are translated in English on the following page: the deities take the majuscule, the numerous'mothers'-miniscule.

Latvian	English
Dievs	God
Dieva dēli	sons of God
Saule	sun
Saules meitas	daughters of Sun
Pērkons	deity of thunder
Pērkona dēli	sons of Thunder
Debess būtnes	Celestial beings
Debess	sky
Laima	deity of fate
Māra	deity of all things material
Mira Māra	deity of the dead (Veļi)
Zeme	Earth
<u>Mātes</u>	<u>the Mothers</u>
zemes	of the earth
jūras (yūras)	of the sea
ūdens	of the water
lietus	of the rain
vēja (vēya)	of the wind
meža	of the forests
veļu	of the Veļi
etc.	etc.

Pērkons, Sons of Dievs, Daughters of Saule

To introduce the category of Dainas that relates to rain/water and thunder, two examples follow where the participation of the celestial deities, such as Pērkons, sons of Dievs, and the daughters of Saule, is dominant.

Latvian

English

33711

Perkons brauca pār jūriņu-
Lietiņš lija jūriņā;
Arājs lūdza Pērkonīti :
Brauc, Pērkoni, šai zemē,
Brauc, Pērkoni, šai zemē-
Miežam asni novītuši.

Pērkons rode across the sea-
A gentle rain fell into the sea;
Arājs called upon dear Pērkons:
Come, Pērkons, to this land,
Come, Pērkons, to this land-
The barley sprouts have wilted.

Kr. Barons and A.Lord have classified the above Daina as a ritual chant invoking sympathetic magic. The external form is presented by the chant in which the singer 'arājs' invites Pērkons (thunder) to bring the rain. The characteristic of the chant is similar to incantations or to prayers, with the symbolic sense in the metonymic expression 'Pērkons', representing the rain. However, the chant has a deeper meaning. The word 'arājs' (pronounced 'arāys') has an archaic signification – he is someone who possesses the art (skill) for the cultivation of the soil. As such, 'arājs' represents also the archetypal provider of food for himself and others. Pērkons can be seen as the provider of rain/water to nourish the earth, thus promoting the fertility and growth of the land.[16]

The following Daina consists of two quatrains and may be considered as a riddle. The first quatrain contains a question, the second provides an answer. However, the interpretation presents a problem.

Latvian	English
33818	
Kas varēja grožus vīt-	Who could weave reins-
No straujā ūdentiņa?	From the swift water?
Kas varēja vilnu cirpt-	Who could shear wool-
No pelēka akmentiņa?	From the small grey stone?
Dieva dēli grožus vija-	The sons of Dievs wove the reins-
No straujā ūdentiņa;	From the swift water;
Saules meitas vilnu cirpa-	The daughters of Saule sheared the wool-
No pelēka akmentiņa.	From the small grey stone.

In the Dainas the sons of Dievs and the daughters of Saule are active either in the sky or on the earth and, therefore, the second quatrain may provide two answers:

As a first interpretation, the sons of Dievs weave the reins from the swiftly flowing brook and the daughters of Saule shear the wool, that is, melting the snow from a small grey stone. This situation may occur in spring, when there is still some snow on the stones and spring water is running in adjacent brooks. Another interpretation may be that the activities of the sons of the Dievs and the daughters of Saule take place in the sky during a thunderstorm with snow - the grey stone being a cumulus cloud.

The first interpretation seems, for its simplicity, to be the correct one, as it serves as an answer posed by the riddle. Within the confines of the theme, it is not important which of the answers is the right one. Of significance is the function of the grey stone that represents one of the important key words, further described in the following Dainas.

The Selection of Dainas Used for the Comparative Analysis

Dievs, Pērkons, Māra

The following examples of Dainas contain the activities of Dievs, 'Dieviņš' (diminutive of Dievs), Pērkons (thunder), Pērkonītis (diminutive of Pērkons), and Māra (Mother Earth), all associated with the circulation of rain/water. These Dainas are used for the comparative analysis with the Vedic hymns. The lines in each quatrain that contain the names of deities, their functions, the pertinent metaphoric expressions, as well as the means of delivery used in the circulation of rain/water, from the celestial vault to the earth, are underlined.

Dievs in the Dainas is portrayed as the carrier of the verdure for grass, as well as the provider of atmospheric conditions required for the pollination of rye fields. After his departure, the rye field is covered with a grey or golden shroud. (Rye bread constitutes the basic food for people in the northern regions of Europe.)

Dievs (God)

Latvian	English
34067	
1. Kas tas bija, kas atjāja -	Who was that, who came riding-
2. Ar akmens kumeliņu?	With a colt of stone?
3. Tas atnesa kokiem lapas,	He brought the leaves for the trees,
4. Zemei zaļu dāboliņu.	The green clover for the earth.
variant 5	
2. Ar pelēku mētelīti?	With a grey mantle?
variant 6	
1. Pa zālīti Dieviņš brauca -	Dear Dievs rode over the grass-
2. Akmenāju kumeliņu;	With a colt of stone;

32533

1. Dieviņš brida rudzu lauku -
2. Ar pelēku mētelīti;
3. Kad izbrida, tad apsedza
4. Pelēkām vārpiņām.

Dear Dievs crossed the rye field-
Clad in a grey mantle;
After the crossing, he covered it
With the grey ears.

S. 233, variants

1. Dieviņš jāja rudzu lauku-
2. Ar akmeņa kumeliņu;
3. Pelēks bija rudzu lauks,
4. Pelēks Dieva kumeliņš.

Dear Dievs rode over the rye field-
With a colt of stone;
Grey was the rye field,
Grey the colt of Dievs.

32535

1. Dieviņš jāja rudzu lauku-
2. Ar pelēku mētelīti;
3. Redzēj' manu rudzu lauku
4. Zelta vilni viļņojot

Dear Dievs rode over the rye field-
With a grey mantle;
I saw my rye field
Undulate in a wave of gold

The Role of Pērkons

The activities of Pērkons are similar to those of Dievs, however, they are more closely associated with the circulation of the rain/water. The bloated goatskin bottle, mare of lead, and the red horses are the metaphoric expressions signifying rain/water.

4147

1. Pērkonītis rucināja
2. Visu garu vasariņu;
3. Atsūtīja zaļu zāli,
4. Dāboliņu pušķotāju.

Dear Pērkons rumbled-
During the long summer;
Sending the green grass,
The flowering clover.

54875

1. Pērkonam visa zeme-
2. Man deviņi bāleliņi;
3. Šķir, Dieviņ, lietus tūci
4. Deviņiem gabaliem

Pērkons owns all the land-
I have nine dear brothers;
Split, dear Dievs, the boil of rain,
Into nine pieces

47708

1. Pieci dēli Pērkonam-
2. Visi pieci rucināja;
3. Divi kala, divi spēra,
4. Piektais rasu birdināja.

Pērkons has five sons-
All five rumbled;
Two forged, two stroke,
The fifth sprayed the dew.

33712

1. Pērkons jāja svina ķēvi -	Pērkons rode a mare of lead-
2. Gar jūrmalu ģeirodams;	Striking along the littoral;
3. Jūrmalā dzelzu stabi,	On the littoral are iron posts,
4. Tur tu vari kapāties.	There you can knock your hoofs.

33705

1. Pērkonam melni zirgi -	Pērkons has black horses-
2. Ar akmeni nobaroti;	Nourished with stone;
3. Dzer sudraba ūdentiņu	They drink water of silver
4. Tēraudiņa silītē.	From a cask of steel.

Māra (Mother Earth)

With the fertile rain/water received from the celestial vault, Māra harvests, protects, and preserves nourishment for all life forms on the earth. Māra is also the preserver and caretaker of water and milk at her sources, and she protects the rye field with a golden ribbon.

32547

1. Kas apjoza zelta jostu	Who encircled the golden ribbon
2. Apkārt manu rudzu lauku?	Around my rye field?
3. Mīļā māra apjozusi	Dear Māra has encircled it
4. Jāņu nakti staigājot.	While walking on the night of "Jāņi" (summer solstice).

32534

1. Dieviņš jāja rudzu lauku -	Dear Dievs rode over the rye field-
2. Ar pelēku mētelīti;	With a grey mantle;
3. Pretīm jāja mīļā Māra -	Towards him rode dear Māra-
4. Šeit būs laime pļāvējam.	Good luck will come to the harvester.

(Brastins: 105)

1. Mīļā Māra, Piena māte -	Dear Māra, Mother of Milk-
2. Dod man tavu labumiņu;	Give me your goodness;
3. Lai pieniņš govīm tek -	May the milk flow from the cows-
4. Kā no Māras avotiņa.	As if from the source of Māra.

33669

1. Grib Dieviņš šo zemīti -	Dear Dievs wants this dear land-
2. Ar ūdeni slīcināt;	Inundate with water;
3. Mīļā Māra Dievu lūdza -	Dear Māra prayed to Dievs-
4. Ap galviņu glāstīdama.	By caressing his gentle head.

The Circulation of Rain/Water

A model of the path of rain/water, from the celestial sea to Mother Earth, (Māra) is represented in Figure 4. The division between the various functions of the celestial and terrestrial deities are represented schematically. Dievs is shown, together with Pērkons and Ūsiņš, as the providers of rain and water for the earth. The wind, known as 'Vēja Māte' (Mother of Wind) represents the atmospheric conditions indispensable for the pollination of rye fields, thus assuring nourishment (rye bread) for its inhabitants. The rain/water is received and protected by Māra (Mother Earth), who is responsible for the maintenance of all life - humans, animals, and plants. The Daina (1872 v.2) on page 61 shows the liason and interdependence between all living beings on earth.

Figure 4

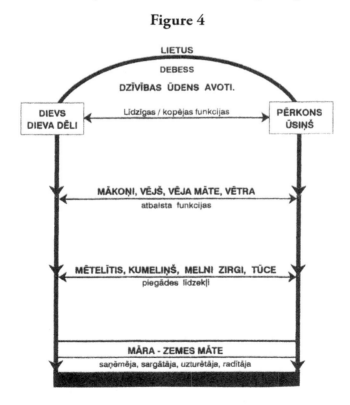

This model represents the movement of rain/water from the celestial deities, via the supporting intermediaries and the various means of delivery, bringing the rain/water from the celestial vault to the earth.

Figure 4 (continued)

Latvian	English
lietus	rain
debess	sky
dzīvības ūdens avoti	sources of the vital fluid
Līdzīgas/kopējas funkcijas	Similar/common functions
Debess būtnes	Celestial beings
Dievs	Dievs (God)
Dieva dēli	sons of Dievs
Pērkons	thunder
Ūsiņš	"Ūsiņš" (deity of horses)
Atbalsta funkcijas	Supportive functions
mākoņi	clouds
vējš (pron. vēysh)	wind
vēja Māte	Mother of wind
vētra	storm
Piegādes līdzekļi	Means of delivery
mētelītis	mantle
kumeliņš	colt
melni zirgi	black horses
tūce (lietus)	boil of rain
Māra	Mother Earth
saņēmēja	receiver
sargātāja	protector
uzturētāja/radītāja	maintenance/creator

The Mantle, the Stone, the Colt of Stone

The significance of the names of the deities, the atmospheric conditions, and the objects of delivery, found in the preceding Dainas and shown in the model, raise some questions and require further elaboration. The functions of the deities and the means of delivery are well defined, however, the sense of each of the terms (names) remain rather obscure. A similar situation, even though the deities that are mentioned do not always have the same names, can also be found in the Vedic hymns.

First, to clarify the situation, the common characteristics of the activities of the celestial deities are as follows:

- They are always the deities, such as 'Dievs', 'Pērkons', and 'Ūsiņš', who are riding the colts (horses) and crossing the rye fields in a grey mantle.
- The mantles, the stones, and the colts of stone are always grey or golden.
- The mantle always covers the entire rye field.

The celestial deities always bring:

- The grey or golden ears to the rye field
- The green grass
- The leaves to the trees, etc.

Second, from all these common characteristics, the presence of the 'stone colt' is the most enigmatic, the significance and the function of 'stone' in particular. A possible answer lies in the search and comparison of the respective cognats of the related Balto-Slavic and Sanscrit languages as in the following example:

Stone:
Latvian: akmens, arch. akmons
Lithuanian: akmuo
Russian: kamen
Sanscrit: asman
PIE: *ak-men, *ak-mon

In Sanskrit 'asman' contains a number of meanings, such as 'the stone', 'the cloud', 'cloud of rain', 'celestial stone', and 'sky'.

In Latvian there are also Dainas with expressions of 'dābolainu kumeliņu' (the clover-spotted colt) and 'spangainu kumeliņu' (brightly spotted colt) -- Daina 32931, var. 1,2, Barons V: 110. In Sanskrit we find a similar term 'prishati', which literally means 'spotted', but is used as a substantive to designate an animal; it is translated in English as 'spotted deer or horse' by Müller, signifying 'rain clouds'. (Mandala 1, H37, note 1, Muller: 63-70). In the paragraph above, 'the stone' in Sanskrit is identified also as 'the cloud' or 'the cloud of rain'. Therefore, 'the stone', 'the colt of stone', and 'the spotted horse' (or deer) have acquired a common meaning – ''the cloud(s) of rain''.

In addition, the Sanscrit expressions 'prishat–asvati' and 'asu – asvati' designate also the celestial deity(ies) Marut(s) (Müller: 70). These Sanskrit expressions have the Latvian cognat Ūsiņš (deity of horses), whose activities are often mentioned in the Dainas. E. Dumézil has interpreted the Sanscrit 'asva' as signifying 'the horse' (Dumezil: 250). *"Moreover, the word is also extended to deities such as the divine twins of Indic religion, the Asvins, and the Gaulish goddess Epona".* (Mallory: 119).

Metathesis

Morphological analysis easily identifies the meaning of the term 'stone'. It entails a diachronic linguistic process, the morphophonetic changes – metathesis (inversion of sounds) – that are often encountered among the Balto-Slavic languages: Latvian: <u>akm</u>ens, arch. <u>akm</u>ons

Russian: <u>kam</u>en
Sanscrit: <u>asm</u>an (the celestial stone)
PIE: *<u>akm</u>en, *<u>akm</u>on

By the inversion of sounds, and following the rules of metathesis, from the archaic Latvian '<u>akm</u>ons' (a stone), a similar word '<u>māk</u>ons' (a cloud) is obtained. By replacing the word '<u>akm</u>ons' with '<u>māk</u>ons' in the appropriate Dainas, their meanings can be deciphered. The Dainas are thus easily understood, that is: the celestial deities that arrive with the clouds, such as nimbus (dispersed clouds), cirrus (spotted clouds), cumulus (heavy dark clouds), or the overcast sky, all bring with them the vital substance (water) to assure growth on earth. The semantic approach and the morphological analysis have contributed to the deciphering of the obscure meanings of <u>the stone</u>, <u>the colt of stone</u>, and <u>the grey mantle (overcast sky)</u>, by discovering the common meanings of these terms. The message contained in the Dainas makes it easy to perceive the atmospheric phenomena observed in nature. The clouds of rain exhibit a mirror image that resembles the grey stones and rock plains disseminated on the surface of the earth (for more examples of metathesis refer to the Notes at the back).[17]

A question remains: what happens after the celestial deities have departed? While crossing the rye field, the celestial deities have covered it with a grey or golden shroud. Two Dainas are presented to illustrate this natural phenomenon, the pollination of the rye field after the departure of the celestial deities. It is signalized by the appearance of a grey or golden shroud covering the entire rye field. Specific atmospheric conditions are required for the event of pollination.

The author himself has only twice observed the phenomenon of pollination, both during his youth in the Latvian countryside. In both cases the late afternoon was calm with a light breeze and drizzle. The entire rye field was covered with a cloud-like grey and translucent shroud, formed by the petals of rye ears, undulating a few meters over the rye stalks. Thus pollination, which lasted only a short time, had occurred. It is best attested by the following Dainas:

Latvian	English
33682	
Lēni, lēni Dieviņš jāja -	Slowly, slowly, dear Dievs was riding-
Pa lielo tīrumiņu;	Across the large field;
Lai vējiņis nenopūta,	So that the light wind does not blow away,
Zaļa zīda mētelīša.	The light mantle (coat) of green silk.

The movement of rain/water is terminated after the land has received the vital fluid and nature is nourished with ripe ears of rye and the green grass. The vital fluid comes under the protection and preservation of the terrestrial deity 'Māra' – Mother Earth. The following Daina pointedly describes the rarely seen process of pollination:

Ciema bērni iztecēja -	The children of the village came running-
Rudzu ziedu raudzīties;	To see the flower (pollen) of rye;
Rudzu zieds gudris bija -	The flower of rye was very cunning -
Tas ielīda vārpiņā.	It slipped into the small ear (of rye).

And so the children from the village did not see the flower of the rye.

Examples of the Results of the Preceding Analysis

On the previous pages the meanings of the enigmatic terms 'mantle', 'stone', and the 'colt of stone' were deciphered and formulated. To illustrate the results, two examples of the Dainas are presented for a comparison: first, the originals with their metaphoric expressions, then the actual meanings of these mytho-poetic verses.

Daina 34067 - original
Latvian   **English**
1. Kas tas bija, kas atjāja-   Who was that, who came riding-
2. Ar akmens kumeliņu?   With a colt of stone?
3. Tas atnesa kokiem lapas,   He brought the leaves for the trees,
4. Zemei zaļu dāboliņu.   The green clover for the earth.

Lines 1. and 2. form a question, with the answer in lines 3 and 4; it was Dievs (God) who came riding with clouds of rain, provided water for the earth, thus making the trees grow and the clover green (lines 3. and 4.).

Daina 34067 – actual meaning
Lines 1 and 2:
    Dievs atnāca   Dievs came
    ar lietus mākoņiem;   with the clouds of rain;
Lines 3 and 4:
    atnesa ūdeni zemei,   brought the water to the earth,
    lai koki un dāboliņš aug.   so that the trees and clover can grow.

Daina 32535 – original
1. Dieviņš jāja rudzu lauku-   Dear Dievs rode over the rye field-
2. Ar pelēku mētelīti;   With a grey mantle;
3. Redzēj' manu rudzu lauku-   I saw my rye field-
4. Zelta vilni viļņojot.   Undulate in a wave of gold.

Lines 1. and 2. contain an observation that a light rain (drizzle) is coming (mantle = overcast sky); and lines 3. and 4. portray what happens afterwards.

Daina 32535 – actual meaning
Lines 1 and 2:
    Dieviņš   Dear Dievs
    atnesa (zemei) ūdeni;   brought the water (to earth);
Lines 3 and 4:
    es redzu mans rudzu lauks   so I see my rye field
    viļņo zelta segā.   undulating in a golden shroud.

The meaning conveyed by the lines 3 and 4 signifies what happens to the rye field after the departure of Dievs. The following event is a precursor to the growth and ripening of the rye field and, ultimately, the harvest of golden rye grains.

When the metaphoric expressions (the enigmatic terms) such as 'colt of stone', 'grey mantle', and 'wave of gold' are replaced with the 'clouds of rain', 'overcast (drizzle) sky', and with the 'undulating golden shroud' (pollination), then the real meanings of the Dainas are revealed.

The Vedic Poetic Material

The Deities of Water, Rain, Wind, and Storm

Chapter 3 (The Vedas) briefly introduced the Vedic texts. Among the multitude of Vedic deities, only those that are mentioned in the hymns associated with the movements of rain/water, are considered. The Vedic hymns of the Rg-veda, which are devoted to the deity Marut(s), are taken from *Der Rig-Veda* by K.F. Geldner and from *Vedic-Hymns* by Max Müller. The hymns devoted to 'Savitar' and to mother 'Earth' are taken from *Hymnes Spéculatifs du Veda*, by Louis Renou. The Rg-veda contains the earliest hymns that were composed by anonymous poets about the time period when the Indo-Europeans (Indic branch of Indo-Iranians) entered the valley of the Indus River (Renou: 59). It can be assumed that the traditional culture of the I.E. immigrants had not yet been overly influenced by the indigenous inhabitants of the Indus Valley, the Dravidian people of the Harrapan culture.

The Deities of the Rg-Veda

First, a short introduction to the Rg-vedic deities that participate in the movement of rain/water are presented.

INDRA is one of the most powerful of the warrior deities and is also known as a symbol of water. Indra's most spetacular heroic act is the killing, in celestial combat, of the demon Vrtra in order to liberate the waters. This episode, the liberation of waters by splitting open the clouds, is considered to be a cosmogonic exploit.

THE MARUT(S) represent an extremely powerful and violent celestial deity(ies). They are the principal providers of water to the 'Mother Earth'. In these activities they are frequently accompanied by the great deity Indra.

PARJANYA, the celestial deity, is associated with the atmospheric movements, such as thunderstorm and lightning. Its name has cognats in the Balto-Slavic languages, such as 'Perun' in the Slavic and 'Pērkons' in the Latvian languages (Karulis II: 39).

THE EARTH, the terrestrial deity, as the universal genetrix and guardian of nourishment, is well presented in the Atharva-veda. Mother Earth is comparable with the deity Māra (Mother Earth) in the Latvian Dainas.

The Circulation of Rain/Water as Described in the Vedic Hymns

The activities of the celestial and terrestrial deities are discussed in this section. The examples (as indicated previously) are taken from the *Der Rig-Veda* by K.F. Geldner, from the *Vedic-Hymns* by Max Müller, and from the *Hymnes Spéculatifs du Veda* by Louis Renou. All these hymns, by anonymous poets, are addressed to the Marut(s) (deity of storms), to the Vayu and Vâta (deities of wind), and to the deity Earth. The identification of the hymns corresponds with their numeration in the above-mentioned publications. The key phrases (metaphoric expressions) and the key words are underlined for each hymn. The translations of the German and French into English are the author's.

Hymns to the Marut(s) and Vayu:
RV5.58.7 (Geldner: p.66)
German
Bei ihrer Fahrt dehnt sich selbst die Erde;
<u>Sie legen ihre Kraft (in sie)</u>
<u>Wie der Gatte den Keim (in die Frau),</u>
Sie haben die <u>Winde als Rosse</u> an die Stange gespannt,
Die Rudra Soehne haben ihren <u>Schweiss zum Regen gemacht.</u>
English
By their voyage the earth itself opened wide;

<u>They placed their own strength (in her)</u>
<u>As a husband the germ (in the wife),</u>
They have harnessed the <u>wind as horses</u> to the yoke,
The sons of Rudra have <u>changed their sweat into rain.</u>

In this hymn the poet begins by describing a cosmic situation; then utilises metaphoric expressions, such as: 'they placed their own strength (the rain) as a husband the germ', 'they have harnessed the wind as horses', to bring the rain. The poet ends the hymn by saying that 'the sons of Rudra have changed their sweat into rain', i.e., they have delivered the rain (water) to the earth.

RV1.168,8. (Geldnerp.246)
German
<u>Die Stroehme jautzen</u> ihren Radschienen entgegen,
wenn diese die <u>Wolkenstimme</u> herforbringen,
Die Blitze loecheln auf die Erde hernieder
<u>Wenn die Marut das Schmalz troeufen.</u>
English
<u>The streams gush forth</u> against their tires (of chariot wheels),
When they send out <u>the voice of the clouds,</u>
The lightnings smiled upon the earth
When the <u>Marut shower down the fatness.</u>

Here the poet immediately begins the hymn with the rain: 'the streams gush forth', 'they send out the voice of the clouds', and ends the hymn with 'the Marut shower down the fatness', i.e., the rain/water down to the earth.

Mandala 1, H85,v5 (Muller: 126, notes 1,2,3)
When you had yoked the <u>spotted deer</u> before your chariots,
<u>hurling</u>[1] the stone (thunderbolt) in the fight,
then <u>the streams of the red-(horse)</u>[2] <u>rush forth</u>:
<u>like a skin</u>[3] <u>with water they water the earth.</u>

After an introduction in the first two lines, the poet ends the hymn with two metaphoric expressions: 'the streams of the red-(horse) rush forth' - the water - , and 'like a skin with water they water the earth'.

RV, 5.54.8. (Müller: 326)

The men with their steeds, like conquerors of clans,
Like Aryaman the Maruts, carrying waterskins,
Fill the well; when the strong ones roar,
They moisten the earth with the juice of sweetness.

RV 5.58.8. (Geldner: p. 65)

German

Hoerst, ihr Herren Marut, seid uns barmherzig,
Ihr viel schenkenden, unsterblicher, des Rechten kundigen,
Die Wahrheit erhoerenden, jugendlichen Seher,
Von hohen Berge stammend hoch wachsend.

English

Hark, you heroes Marut, be gracious to us,
You of great bounty, immortal, righteous,
Beholders of truth, young prophets,
Dwelling on mighty mountains, and grown mighty.

In this hymn, the relationship between the anonymous poet and the deity Marut are portrayed. The praising of the deity Marut is overwhelming with a subtle suggestion of reciprocity, e.g., by glorifying the deity, the poets expect a return in kind.

The principle of reciprocity is well expressed in the following hymn (RV1,87.2., Müller: 159). The poet, for his verbal oblations, expects from the deity Marut 'the honey-like fatness' - the rain – 'for him who praises you'. The principle of reciprocity is also subtly invoked in the hymn RV XII-63 (Renou: 202) later on.

RV1, 87.2. Müller: 159

When you have seen your way through the clefts, like birds,
O, Maruts, on whatever road it be, then the casks (clouds)
On your chariots trickle everywhere, and you pour out
The honey-like fatness (the rain) for him who praises you.

RV.11.38.2, Savitar (Renou: 21)

Français

Lui le Dieu haut dressé ; afin que tout lui obéisse
il tend au loin les deux bras, (le dieu) aux larges mains,

Les eaux elles-mêmes sont assujetties à ses ordonnances
le vent lui-même s'arrête en son circuit.
English
The god highly admired; for all who obey him
He extends his two arms, (the God) with large hands.
The waters themselves are subjected to his decrees
The wind itself stops in its course.

The Earth

The hymns containing references to the Earth are presented below. They are taken from the section 'La Terre' (the Earth) in *Hymnes Speculatifs du Veda* by Louis Renou (Renou: 189-202). **The metaphoric expressions and key words are underlined in each hymn.**

Français
Atharva-Veda, XII, 1 (AV XII – 1)
Haute Vérité, Ordre formidable, Consécration,
Ardeur, Formule, Sacrifice – supportent la Terre,
Maitresse de ce qui fut et de ce qui sera,
veuille la Terre nous faire un vaste domaine….
English
The Great Verity, Formidable Order, Consecration,
Ardour, Formula, Sacrifice – support the Earth
The Maitresse of that what was and will be,
would the Earth create for us an immense domain.

AV XII – 12
Français
Ce qui est ton milieu, ô Terre, ton nombril,
ces forces nourricières qui sont nées de ton corps,
mets-les en notre possession, purifie-nous!
La Terre est une mère, je suis fils de la Terre,
mon père est Parjanya, qu'il nous comble!
English
That what is your milieu, oh Earth, your navel,
the nourishing forces that are born in your body,
put them in our possession, purify us!

The Earth is a mother, I am a son of the Earth,
my father is Parjanya, who fulfils us!

AV XII – 17
Français
Mère des plantes, universelle génitrice,
vaste Terre solide, que soutien la Loi,
douce, favorable, puissions-nous vivre le long d'elle toujours!
English
Mother of plants, the universal genetrix,
Immense, solid Earth, sustained by the Law,
gentle, favourable, could we live along with her forever!

AV XII – 42
Français
Elle sur qui est la nourriture, le riz et l'orge,
À qui appartiennent ces cinq établissements,
la Terre dont Parjanya est l'époux,
et que la pluie engraisse, - hommage soit à elle!
English
She, on whom is the nourishment, the rice and barley,
to her belong the five establishments,
the Earth, whose husband is Parjanya,
and that the rain fattens, - pay homage to her !

AV XII – 57
Français
Comme un cheval (secouant de lui) la poussière, la Terre a secoué
les peuples qui dès sa naissance ont résidé sur elle, -
(la Terre) harmonieuse, avant-courrière, gardienne du monde,
mainteneuse des arbres et des plantes.
English
As a horse (shedding off) the dust, the Earth has shaken
the peoples who, since their birth have resided on her, -
(the Earth) harmonious, the fore-runner, guardian of people,
preserver of the trees and plants.

AV XII – 63
Français
<u>O Terre, o mère,</u> dépose moi
d'heureuse manière, que je sois bien installé!
En harmonie avec le ciel, <u>o Poète</u>
<u>mets – moi dans la fortune, dans la prospérité!</u>
English
<u>Oh, Earth, o mother,</u> settle me
in a happy manner, so that I am well accommodated!
In the harmony with the sky, <u>oh Poet</u>
<u>put – me in fortune, in prosperity!</u>

The Comparative Analysis

The Circulation of the Vital Fluid as Presented in the Two Poetic Corpuses

The examples of Dainas and Vedic hymns that contain references to rain, water, and storm were presented in the previous sections. These mytho-poetic verses were chosen because they describe the circulation of rain/water from the celestial vault to the earth. Water, as substance, represents the vital common element indispensable for all life forms and for all human cultures around the world. The Dainas and Vedic hymns describe the daily observations of celestial and terrestrial events and phenomenons, as seen by the Indo-Europeans during their migrations. The circulation of rain/water, as described in the Dainas, is schematically presented in Figure 4, and similarly, in the Vedic hymns in Figure 5.

In general, by comparing the texts of the Dainas and Vedic hymns, the parallels and similarities become obvious. The descriptions of the movement of water by the celestial deities down to mother Earth are similar in the Dainas and Vedic hymns. The means employed in rain/water circulation by the participating deities are also similar. However, the cosmogonic aspects in the Dainas and Vedic hymns are not discussed here, as the poets have tended to invent fictitious cosmogonic events. The focus instead is on the analysis and comparison of the mytho-poetic verses in which the celestial and terrestrial deities are participating in the circulation of rain/water.

The Celestial Beings

In the Dainas, Dievs is mentioned most often. Some of the same functions, such as the 'riding on the colt of stone' are performed also by Pêrkons – the deity of thunder, and by 'Ûsiņš' – the deity of horses. In the Vedas, the substantive Dyaus, also Devah(cognat Dievs in Latvian and God in English), is infrequently used, whereas the other deities, Maruts in particular, are encountered often. Of interest is that the activities of Dievs, Pêrkons, and Ūsiņš in the Dainas are traditionally pacific, whereas those of Maruts in the Vedic hymns are belligerant and violent. An explication for these differences could be that the Dainas were anonymously and collectively created, then reduced and polished into their final form as quatrains, perhaps over thousands of years. On the other hand, the Vedic hymns were composed by anonymous poets (individuals) who have extracted the ideas from the oral tradition (Indo-European) and then sumptuously embellished them to please and venerate the omnipotent gods, hoping to receive favours in return. Such expressions and ideas cannot be found in the Dainas. The contents of the Vedic hymns are characterized by L. Renou: *"d'ailleurs les poètes se sont arrêtés de préférence au schéma cosmogonique"* (Renou: 10). The fact that the Vedic hymns were written by anonymous poets is evidenced in a number of hymns, for example, Mandala V, H 58,v.8, where the poets supplicated the Maruts to listen to their words.

The Terrestrial Beings

In the Vedic hymns the receiver of the vital fluid is identified as Mother Earth. In the Dainas the deity Māra, known also as Mother Earth, possesses the same functions and is also assisted by numerous Mothers to take care of and preserve life on the earth. The paths and the means of delivery used in the circulation of the vital fluid are, generally, the same in the Dainas as in the Vedic hymns.

The Cognats: the Names and Words

In addition to the global parallelism, encountered in the process of cosmic circulation, between the Dainas and Vedic hymns, a number of important names and terms also have cognats in the two languages:

Dievs corresponds to **Dyaus**, the celestial Vedic God
Pērkons corresponds to **Parjanya**, both the deities of thunder

Ūsiņš corresponds to **Asvins,** both the deities of horses
akmens (arch. – **akmon),** the **stone** corresponds to the Vedic
asman and to the P.I.E. **akmon**
vējš (pron. vēysh), gen.**vēya** corresponds to the **wind,** and to
the Sanscrit **vayu.**

In addition to the cognats in a strict sense, there are also series of terms
and concepts that correspond well to the 'semantic cognats' as termed by
Watkins. The key words and their most important cognats, together with
the metaphoric expressions (underlined in the verses presented earlier),
which are most often mentioned in the comparative analysis, are taken
from the Latvian Dainas (in Latvian) and from the Vedic hymns (in
English) directly, and enumerated and recapitulated in Table 2 below.

TABLE 2

Note: The names of the celestial and terrestrial deities and the
personifications of natural phenomena are capitalized; in Latvian the
genitive is shown in brackets. The names, words, and the metaphoric
expressions are presented as follows:

- **column 1:** all in Latvian, from the examples of Dainas.

- **column 2, section B:** all in English, from hymns already translated
into English (i.e., Max Muller and K.F. Geldner) and from other hymns
translated from German and French by the author and taken from the
examples of Vedic hymns. The translation and interpretation of the
terms and metaphoric expressions, from Sanskrit into the German,
English, and French, are those of K.F. Geldner, Max Müller, and Louis
Renou, respectively.

The texts between the columns 1 and 2 are not translatable literally;
the metaphoric expressions in Latvian (column 1) are taken from the
examples of Dainas directly and translated into English in the column 3.
The metaphoric expressions in English are taken from the Vedic hymns
directly and presented in column 2. **All the metaphoric expressions
possess a single signification: the rain or water in various stages of
the circulation of the vital fluid.**

-column 3: the translation from Latvian (column 1) into English (column 3) is by the author.

-section C: the translation and interpretation of Sanskrit terms into the French are by Louis Renou, translated into English by the author.

TABLE 2 – Summary

SECTION A: The celestial deities – the providers of the vital fluid

Column 1 Latvian	Column 2 Sanscrit	Column 3 English
Diev-s(a)	Dyaus	God
Pērkon-s(a)	Parjanya	deity of thunder
Ūsiņ-š(a)	Ašvin	deity of horses

SECTION B: The circulation of the vital fluid (rain/water)

Column 1 Latvian	Column 2 Sanscrit, translation	Column 3 English
mākonis	stone	cloud
akmens, akmons	asman, akmon	stone
34067 Akmens kumeliņsPelēks mētelītis	**RV,5.58.7** Husband the germ Sweat into rain	colt of stone grey mantle
S 233, var. Dieva kumeliņš pelēks rudzu lauks	**RV 1, 168.8** streams gush forth voice of clouds	colt of God grey field of rye

32535 pelēks mētelītis zelta vilni viļņojot	RV 1, 85.3 streams of red (horse) skin with water	grey mantle undulate gold wave
4147 Pērkonītis rucināja atsūtīja zaļu zāli	RV 5, 54.8 carrying waterskins juice of sweetness	rumbling thunder sending green grass
33705 Pērkonam melni zirgi Ar akmeni nobaroti	RV 1, 87.2 casks (clouds) honey-like fatness	Thunder has black horses nourished with stone

SECTION C: Terrestrial deities – reception of the vital fluid

Column 1 **Latvian**	Column 2 **Sanskrit, translation**	Column 3 **English**
Māra	deity Earth	Māra (Mother Earth)
The Functions		
saņēmēja barotāja aizsargataja uzturetaja	genitrix nourishment guardian maintenance	beneficiary provider protector preserver

Note: A prototype model for the Latvian deities, which participate in the circulation of rain/water, including their functions, was shown in Figure 4. A similar model showing the activities of the Vedic deities is presented on the Figure 5, next page.

Figure 5
THE RAIN/WATER

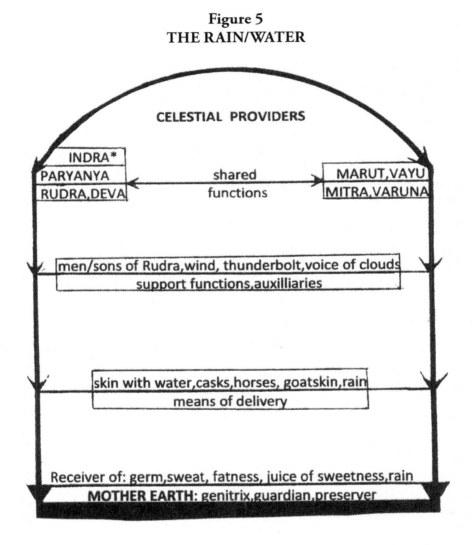

*Model of the Vedic celestial and terrestial deities, the
auxilliaries, and the means of delivery of the vital fluid.
deity, symbolising water

CHAPTER 5: THE BROADENED MAIN THEME OF THE MONOGRAPH

The main theme are broadened by two subthemes to confirm the positive results of the comparative analysis between the Latvian Dainas and the Vedic hymns. To begin, the main theme of the monograph is recalled: *The research presented in the monograph dealt with the question of the similarities and parallelism found in the Latvian Dainas and in the Vedic hymns.*

The comparative analysis between the mytho-poetic material, the Latvian Dainas, and the Vedic hymns, confirmed that surprisingly close similarities and parallelism do exist. These conclusions were based on mytho-linguistic research methods. However, it is commonly known that a singularly linguistic approach may not give a convincing answer. Other scientific disciplines, such as archaeology, geography, and history should be involved to confirm and complement the linguistic research results. This is of particular importance when the origin of the research material is historically separated by some 1000 years (the time of separation of Indo-Iranians from Proto-Balts, circa 2500 BC, and their arrival in Indus Valley, 1500 BC), and geographically by a distance of 6000 km.

What are the salient points that would bridge the historical time spread and the great geographical distance? One of them is the geographical location of the Danubian basin in Europe (west of the Black Sea) and its cultural environment. Another point is the fact that all the migratory routes of the Indo-Europeans, except the Proto-Baltic branch, coming from Eastern Europe, had to cross the territory of the Danubian basin before spreading into the Balkans. By crossing the Aegean Sea, the Indo-Europeans entered Anatolia and the Middle East and, most likely, continued along the seaboard of Persian Gulf and Arabian Sea to the Indus Valley.

The Danubian Scene

The Danubian scene may be viewed as a `prehistorical melting pot` of various races, social structures, and languages. In the early Mezolithic

Europe was inhabited by semi-nomadic fisher-hunters and gatherers, as far north as the Baltic region. Traces of early settlers have been found near lake Burtnieks in northern Latvia circa 9000 BC (Latvijas: 50-53). The Danubian region changed during the early Neolithic (ar. 7000 BC) when agricultural settlements appeared and with them a matriarchal social structure evolved. In the fourth millenium BC the first Indo-Europeans, the Kurgan people, known as Celts, Greeks, perhaps Italics, and Anatolians arrived and settled in the Danubian region, before they dispersed south and south-west. The migration of the Northern branch (Corded Ware horizon) of the Indo-Eurpeans, the Indo-Iraniens and the Germano-Slavic-Baltic (Proto-Baltic) peoples, reached the Danubian scene as late as the third millenium BC. The Proto-Baltic peoples dispersed west (Germanic) or remained (Slavic and Baltic) in their arrival regions along and south of the Baltic sea. The Indo-Iranians turned south and entered the Danubian region where, most probably, they encountered the remnants of the earlier Indo-European migrants, the Kurgan people. The significance of the Danubian cultural scene, the crossroads of all Indo-European migrants, exept the Proto-Balts, is well defined by J. P. Mallory:

> *"We may anticipate then that both the Corded Ware horizon and the Balkan-Danubian complex are essential to any explanation of the origin of the Indo-Europeans of Europe. Both the specific character of these different cultures and the problem of their ultimate origins – be they indigenous or intrusive – will be the topics of Chapter Eight when we attempt to trace the expansion of the Indo-Europeans. Before we can do this we shall have to abandon our historical evidence and seek from other sources what the earliest I.E. held in common."* (Mallory: 109).

From Europe to the Indus Valley

The main theme of the monograph deals with two mytho-poetic corpuses: the Latvian Dainas and the Vedic hymns. Therefore, an inquiry into movements of the ancient Latvians (Proto-Baltic branch) and Indo-Iranians (Indic branch) is pursued. It is well known that the ancient Latvians remained in the lands they entered, the eastern shores of the Baltic sea, and still continue to speak their ancient language. The situation of the

Indo-Iranian people and their language is more complex and intensively argued among linguists and historians. Therefore, later in the text, a new hypothesis is proposed to outline the itinerary the Indo-Iranians followed to reach India, after they separated from the Proto-Baltic branch.

The Arrival of the Indo-Europeans in Europe

The origin of the Indo-European peoples remains in prehistoric obscurity. As a language community, some 200 years ago, they first acquired the name of `Indo-Germanisch` (Indo-Germanic) and later that of Indo-Europeans. Their movements from the euro-asiatic steppes into Europe are relatively well traced by the archeological finds. The first migrants, the Kurgan (tumulus) people, entered the Danubian basin by following the northern plains of the Black Sea littoral, circa 3500 BC. (Gimbutas 3: XX). Progressively, all Europe was penetrated by various consecutive movements. The arrival of the Corded Ware culture in the Baltic region is the last significant movement of the Indo-European people in Europe. They are represented by two major language groups, the Indo-Iranian and the Proto-Baltic branches, as shown on the cladistic language tree (Figure 1). The geographical situation of the epoch is shown on Map 3. At the time of the arrival of the Indo-Europeans, Europe was not devoid of indigenous people. In the Danubian basin, the culture named 'Danubian', had already flourished for some 4000 years, from the seventh to the third millenium BC. The Danubian river basin covers an immense territory: from its sources in South Germany, crossing Austria and the Balkans before reaching the Black Sea in Romania. The basin is characterized by rich soil well suited for agriculture, and was cultivated by people known as the `Danubian farmers`. The region has acquired the name of `Old Europe` or `The Civilisation of ancient Europe`, a name given by M. Gimbutas (Gimbutas 2: XVI). The fluid adjacent borders of the expansive Danubian culture, extending south from the Adriatic sea and north to the Baltic sea, are shown on Map 3, next page.

After the arrival of the Indo-Europeans, a new and hybrid culture was created by the indigenous people and the new entrants. Since there is no evidence of a massive invasion of historical proportions, it can be assumed that the penetration of the Indo-Europeans into Europe was relatively slow and of varied intensity. After many centuries of transculturation, the area saw a genesis of a language community named `macro-balte` by B. Sergent, and according to Sergent: ``*cela signe l`apparition du groupe macro-balte dans l`histoire*``(Sergent: 92). The linguistic expanse of the macro-baltic group, which approximately coincides with an area represented by Baltic river names, is shown on Map 4 (Gimbutas: 130-131).

Map 3
(Mallory: 109)

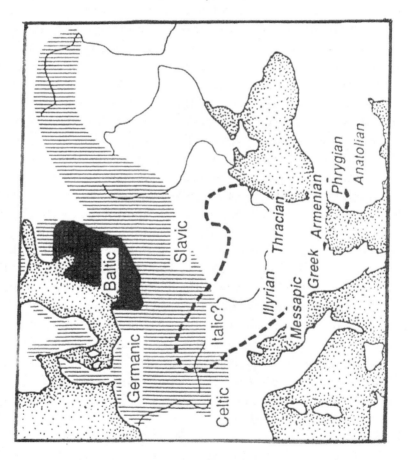

Most of the Indo-European languages of Europe and Anatolia may be traced back to the earlier territories of the Corded Ware horizon (indicated by vertical hatching) and the Balkan-Danubian complex (dotted line).The blackened territory (drawn by the author) shows the reduced habitat of the ancient Baltic tribes circa 1200 AD.

Map 4
The Balts: Linguistic and Historic Background

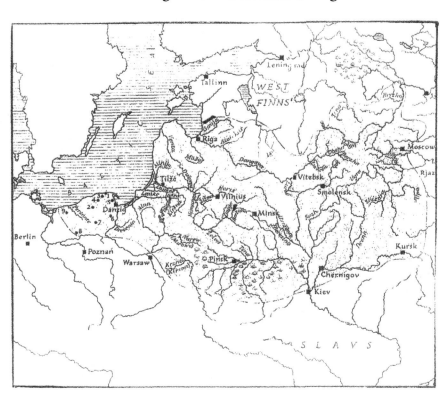

The area of the Baltic river names.

The Origin and Evolution of the Danubian Culture

The first traces of Danubian culture, circa 7000 BC, are found on the shores of the Aegean sea. By 3000 BC, the Danubian culture has gradually expanded across Europe from West to East. It constituted the borders of the Old Europe.

Where is the origin of the people of Old Europe? Where do they come from? It is known that the knowledge (art) of soil cultivation came from the Middle-East, by crossing Anatolia, Greece and the Balkans. This hypothesis is based on the archaeological finds desribed in *The Language of the Goddess* by Marija Gimbutas (Gimbutas: 3).

Consequently, it can also be presumed that these tillers of soil arrived in the basin of the Danube river by the same route, from the south-east. After encountering the semi-nomadic autochtones of the region, and by the process of transculturation, a new hybrid culture evolved – known as the Danubian culture. The three fundamentals that characterize the Danubian culture are: the intensive agriculture, the matriarchal social structure, and the cosmogonic concept of the Great Goddess. M. Gimbutas has decoded and interpreted the various semiotic configurations found on the feminine statuettes (bone or ceramic), and has confirmed that these configurations represent a veritable semiotic language. That language is the only message left for the posterity of the Danubian culture.

It can be assumed that by the way of diffusion, the cultural traits of the Danubian social structure can also be found in the Baltic cultural environment. Without going into details, only the symbolic significations of lines and signs, painted on the feminine statuettes, and relatives to the aquatic sphere, are presented in the monograph. Evidently, the aquatic sphere signifies the source of life itself – the water. Some examples of the semiotic language are presented on the next page (Figure 6).

FIGURE 6

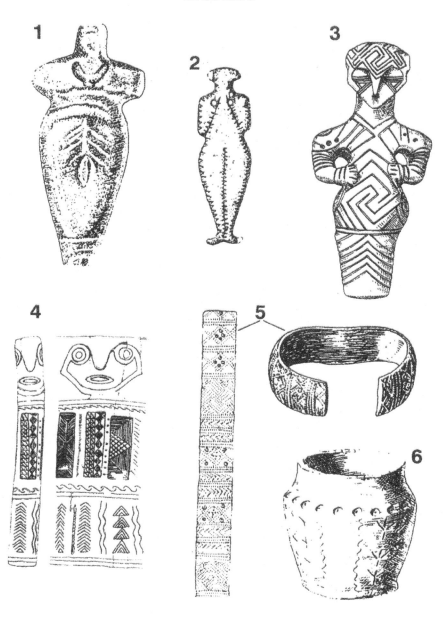

The identification of these objects is found on the next page.

Legend

1. Feminine figure, bone plaque, Neolithic, Trente-Italie, (Gimbutas 3: 103).
2. Feminine figure, bone plaque, beginning of the Neolithic, Sārnate-Latvia(Latvijas: 33)
3. Feminine figure (Deesse), ceramic, beginning of the Neolithic, Vrsac-Balcans, (Gimbutas 3: 12).
4. Figure Deesse – owl, bone plaque, Neolithic, Gaban Trente – Italie, (Gimbutas: 3: 70).
5. Bronze bracelet, iron age, Vilkamuiža – Latvia. (Latvijas: 48, tabula).
6. Ceramic vase, iron age, Geistauti – Latvia, (Latvijas: 40, tabula).

Danubian agricultural knowledge expanded along the tributaries of the Danube river, where the soil was well suited for agriculture and the waterways for transportation and communications. The Danubian culture, by its expansion, influenced the far-reaching lands of the Old Europe. There are no written historical witnesses (in the conventional sense) of the expansion and diffusion of Danubian culture. Its traits are encoded by the signs and symbols on a multitude of feminine statuettes of various shapes and forms found in archeological excavations throughout the Balkans and Eastern Europe. These signs and symbols show surprising similarities (Fig. 6, objects 4, 5, 6). It is impossible to determine if these similarities represent a uniquely local creation or wether they came, partially or entirely, borrowed from the Danubian culture.

Archeological finds confirm that the Baltic region has been inhabited by fishermen, hunters, and gatherers since the Mezolithic. From 4000 to 2000 BC, their social structure has been matrifocal (egalitarian), but after 2000 BC became patrifocal (Latvijas: 50-51). This change coincides with the arrival of the Indo-Europeans.

The Matriarchy and the Vital Fluid

In southeastern Europe the presence of a matriarchy in Neolithic is confirmed by the numerous feminine statuettes found in Italy, the Balkans, and further north in Latvia (Fig. 6, objects 1, 2, 3, 4). The signs and symbols on these statuettes are interpreted as the graphic representations of the forces and revelations observed in the nature, in the form of zigzags, undulating lines, meanders, chevrons, rhombes, etc. These signs and symbols, in particular the zigzags and meanders, which are painted on various objects and the feminine statuettes, characterize the Danubian culture. They represent the sacred character of water and symbolically associates them with the rivers, brooks, sacred sources of water, and the celestial sphere with rain (Gimbutas, 3: 43). Moreover, these signs and symbols and the feminine statuettes themselves point to a matriarchal social structure pervasive in the daily life, with the omnipotent figure of the Great Goddess. It is not surprising that the aquatic element of the Danubian culture resemble the roles of mother Earth in the Vedic hymns and the deity Māra (mother Earth) in the Latvian Dainas. All the activities of these feminine deities are associated with the conservation and protection of the vital fluid – rain/water.

The Baltic (Latvian and Lithuanian) mythological material contains many of the surviving features of the Danubian social structure. The matrifocal elements are apparent throughout the contents of the quatrains of the Latvian Dainas. Māra represents the archetypal deity, who is responsible for the preservation of all life on earth. Māra is the receiver of the vital fluid as well as the source of the universal genetrix. The divine attributes of Māra have survived many thousands of years since the vanishing – however not entirely - of the Danubian culture. The divine character of mother Earth is mentioned by the roman traveler, historian Tacitus as late as 98 AD, when he writes that a 'mater deum' (the mother of God) is worshiped as the principal deity by the Aiisti (Tacitus: 139) – the people living in the Baltic culture area. These remarks by Tacitus correspond well with the functions of the Great Goddess of the Danubian culture, the archetypal Māra of the Latvian Dainas, and with the Vedic deity mother Earth, as reflected in the Vedic hymns of Atharva-Veda. In the Atharva-Veda mother Earth, as a universal genetrix, is supplicated by the poets as late as the second millennium BC. Of note is, that the matrifocal social structure of the ancient Latvians has survived the aggression of the patriarchal ideology of Christianity and, to some extent, is still observable in contemporary Latvian society.

From Europe to India – The New Hypothesis

Introduction

The enigma of the origin and dispersion of the Indo-Europeans and their languages has persisted for some 150 years. The scientific inquiries of the last 30 years have raised two fundamental questions: one of a historic – linguistic nature and the other of a historic – geographic nature. To answer these two questions, a new hypothesis is proposed. However, before proceding with the new hypothesis, the status of the two language branches, the Indo-Iranian and the Proto-Baltic, is briefly discussed.

The main theme of the monograph deals with two mytho-poetic corpuses: the Latvian Dainas and Vedic hymns. Therefore, an inquiry about the movements of their creators, the Latvians from Proto-Baltic branch and the Indo-Iranians, both belonging to the Corded Ware horizon, is pursued. It is well known that the Latvians remained in the lands they entered, circa 2300 BC, along the southeast shores of the Baltic Sea, where they live today. There is agreement among linguists that the Latvian (Baltic) language, still spoken today, is the most archaic in comparison with other Indo-European languages spoken in Europe. The reasons for this archaism, however, are seldom postulated. Therefore, the migration routes of the Indo-Iranians and their language has become pivotal in order to solve the question of the similarities between the mytho-poetic verses of the Latvian Dainas and Vedic hymns. The new cladistic language tree (Figure 1) shows that the Latvians (Proto Baltic branch) and Indo-Iranians spoke a common Indo-European language. After the separation, about 2500 BC, the Indo-Iranians moved south and entered the Danubian cultural area, where they encountered the remnants of the Kurgan people who had entered the region circa 3500 BC. From there the Indo-Iranians spread southeast into the Balkans and after crossing the Aegean sea entered Anatolia.

The Historio-Linguistic Scene

After the discovery at the beginning of the 20th century of the ruins of the ancient Indus Valley civilization, the prevalent hypothesis regarding the migration of the Indo-European people, was reversed. They did not leave India to migrate, by passing the Aral and Pontic regions, and to settle in Europe. The opposite had taken place - the Indo-Europeans came from West, from Europe, to settle in the Indus Valley. The name itself, the Indo-Europeans, is misoriented for its make-up suggests that their origin would be found among the indigenous population of north-west India.[18]

What is known now and proven by archaeological exploration is that the presence of the first Indo-Europeans in Europe was discovered north of the Black Sea, about the 5th millennium BC, as evidenced by their burial (tumulus) sites. They acquired the name of "Kurgan (tumulus) people", inhabiting the region of lower Dniepr-Volga rivers 4400-4300 BC as dated by M.Gimbutas (Sergent : 403-404). From there they entered the Danubian basin and continued further west and south-west into Central Europe, the Balkans, and Anatolia, respectively. Among the hybridized Kurgan people who spoke a somewhat modified Indo-European language, we find the ancestors of the Celts, Greeks, Anatolians, and probably the Armenians.

While inhabiting Anatolia, the first Indo-Europeans developed the Hittite Civilization and they also became the first Indo-E.uropeans who learned the art of writing (cuneiform). About the end of third millennium BC, the Indo-Iranians entered Anatolia and joined the remnants of the earlier entrants, the Kurgan peoples. After the separation from the Proto-Baltic language branch, the Indo-Iranians crossed the Danubian cultural region, the Balkans, and entered as a culturally hybridized society the Anatolian peninsula. After a relatively short stay in Anatolia, the Indo-Iranians migrated further east into the Mesopotamian cultural area. Not meeting serious resistance by the indigenous people, facilitated by the low coastal terrain, the Indo-Iranians followed the coasts of the Persian Gulf and the Arabian Sea, and in about 1600 BC entered the ancient Persia (Iranian branch) and circa 1500 BC the Indus Valley (Indic branch). They entered Persia and Indus Valley as a hybridized society and with languages altered by the influence of non-Indo-European languages, encountered along the migratory pathways. By contacts with local populations they also left some Indo-European linguistic traces in the Sumerian tribes south and in the adjacent territories ,such as the Mitanni kingdom, north.(Mallory: 38) After the arrival in Indus Valley another process of transculturation with the indigenous people took place, this time with the local people of the Indus Valley civilization (Harrapan). Finally, the original ancient Indo-European language, which was spoken at the time of separation from the Proto-Baltic branch, was not spoken any more. Altered, it has survived only in Sanscrit, however, as a dead language.

The movements of the Indo-Europeans, and the dispersion of their languages in Europe, are shown on Map 5,next page.

Map 5

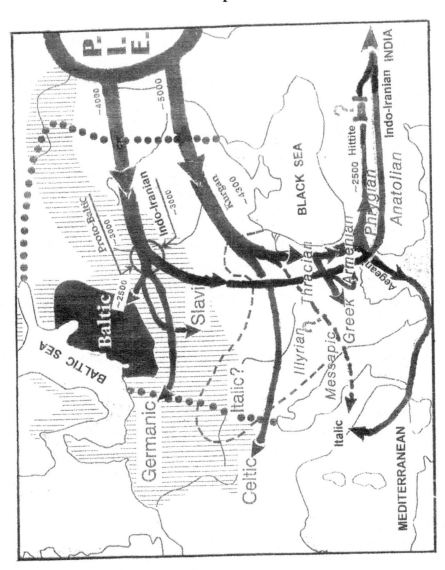

*Migratory pathways of I.E. in Europe; approximate location
(circled) of the separation between the Proto-Baltic and
Indo-Iranian branches(ref.: Figure 1 and Map 3).*

************* -- extent of the Macro-Baltic language, c. 800 BC

The Historical – Geographical Scene

From Europe to Anatolia

The question of the most probable migratory routes that were followed by the Indo-Europeans is expanded and presented by the new hypothesis. They, circa 2500 BC, and apart of those who dispersed in Europe proper, entered Anatolia coming from the Balkans. This itinerary is affirmed by most historians and linguists. To quote B.Sergent:

> ``*Toutes les etudes rigoureuses sur la question de l'origine des Anatoliens montré qu'ils sont originaires de la région balkanique*'' (Sergent: 409). [19]

This assertion is also supported by the indian linguist S.Chatterji:

> ``*Their pathway to Asia Minor, for aught we know, might equally have been through what are now Moldavia, Wallachia and Rumania, and Bulgaria and Thracia, rather than the Caucasus range*`` (Chatterji: 4).

The Anatolians, together with the local autochthonous population (Hatti) and the new entrants of Kurgan peoples created the powerful Hittite Empire. As Hittites they conquered part of Syria, fought Egyptians, plundered Babylon (1530 BC), and by the middle of third millennium BC attacked the kingdom of Assyria.

The Indo-Iranians were the last of I.E. who entered Anatolia, circa 2000 BC, and continua to migrate, for whatever reasons, further east to Lower Mesopotamia. It is not known wether the earlier Indo-European settlers of Anatolia have joined the Indo-Iranians by moving out of Anatolia. Being latecomers, the Indo-Iranians, in all probability formed the core of migrants who continued their journey farther east. They followed the ancient trading routes from Anatolia through Mesopotamia to Indus Valley. There is no evidence of Indo-Iranian settlements in Mesopotamia, therefore their presence there has been of a transient nature. Before the Indo-Iranians reached Lower Mesopotamia, the local Akkad and Sumer kingdoms had been destroyed and their lands pillaged by the Guteens circa 2300 BC, a non-Indo-European

Zagros mountain tribes from the North. This fact may have facilitated the passage of Indo-Iranians through the region for they did not encountered locally organized resistance of historical significance. They followed the ancient coastal trade routes along the Persion Gulf where probably, after the Sraits of Hormuz and at the beginning of the second millennium BC, the Iranian branch separated, entered, and settled in the northeast highland plateau of ancient Persia. The Indic branch of the Indo-Iranians continued along the coast of Arabian Sea and entered the Indus Valley about 1500 BC. It is of utmost significance to mention here that another branch separated from the Indic branch, continued south along the coastal lands of Indian Ocean, and settled, circa 600 BC, on the southernmost island of Ceylon (Sri Lanka) of the Indian continent. They continue to speak an I.E. language called Singhalese.[20] Other Indo-European speaking tribes have settled in the island chain of Maldives, west of the Indian continent. Unfortunately, very little is known about these people, even less of their origin.

A Brief Review

Linguistic Factors

The focus of the main theme of the monograph is centered on the similarities and parallelism between the ancient Latvian Dainas and the Rg-Vedic hymns. The comparative analysis of the mytho-poetic materiel, essentially, was carried out by using linguistic approach. However, it became apparent that a solely linguistic approach could not provide a conclusive answer for a situation where the mytho-poetic materiel is separated by some 1000 years in time and some 6000 km. in distance. On the previous pages the migration pathways of the Indo-European peoples and, consequently, their languages were discussed and graphically presented on the Map 5 and Map 6. It is well known that any language undergoes diachronic changes over time, and that all languages are influenced by migratory pathways through territories where they meet indigenous people speaking different languages – in this case the non-Indo-European speaking peoples. As a result, the Indo-Iranians, when entering the Indus Valley, they no longer spoke their original language – spoken at the time of separation from the Proto-Balts - but a modified version of it. Therefore, it can be postulated that, in the case of Latvian (Proto-Baltic branch) and the Indic (Indo-Iranian branch) languages, the Latvian language is more archaic than the Indic language of the Rg-Vedic hymns. This conclusion is also attested by the fact that the Latvians remained very close to the place of separation from the Indo-Iranian branch and were not exposed to the influences of the non-Indo-European speaking people. Conversely, the Indo-Iranians, while moving from Eastern Europe, entered the hybridized Danubian cultural area, crossed the Balkans and Anatolia and, by continuing through Mesopotamia to the Indus Valley, encountered numerous non I.E. speaking people. As a result the Indic language, as represented by Vedic Sanscrit, contains numerous words and names borrowed from non-I.E.-speaking people.

The Indo-Aryans

In the context of the new hypothesis, the question of the obscure Indo-Aryans and their languages becomes redundant. The plateau of north-east Persia was settled by the Iranians, circa 1600 BC, after the separation from the Indo-Iranian branch. The new hypothesis, based on historic-geographic grounds, presents a simple and comprehensible explanation.

Geographic Factors

From where to where and why? These are everlasting questions when the problem of the movements of an identifiable language community is addressed. The case of the Indo-Europeans, or more precisely – the Proto-Indo-Europeans – has been vexing to historians and linguists for nearly two centuries and yet without a convincing scenario. It is the author's presumption that the geographical and geological factors have not been sufficiently heeded when trying to reconstruct the movements of the Proto-Indo-Europeans. The proposed new hypothesis provides many answers to the dispersal of Proto-Indo-Europeans from their former habitat, as well as the successive migratory pathways of their descendants – the Indo-Europeans - from Eastern Europe to India.

The Proto-Indo-Europeans

Where did the P.I.E. come from? Before entering Europe they have abandoned, partially or entirely, their former habitat in the eastern regions of the Caspian and Aral seas. The most probable reason for the abandonment of their homeland was the gradual disappearance of the grazing lands under the advancing desert sands, the Karakum desert expanse east of the Caspian sea. To the south their passage was blocked by the highest mountain ranges in the world, to the east by the unproductive barren land. An exeption were the P.I.E. speaking Tocharians who followed the ancient Silk Road eastwards. However, most of the P.I.E. moved north and through the Pontic region entered, as Indo-Europeans (I.E.), the lowlands of Eastern Europe. The presence of the P.I.E. in their homeland is attested by the discovery of an ancient settlement on the Amu-Daria River south of the Aral Sea. This region, the origin of the P.I.E., some 3000 years later (ar. 2nd millennium BC) was inhabited by an agglomeration of various separate cultural groups and identified as the Andronovo cultural area. More information on the Andronovo and Indo-Iranian cultural identities is found in Mallory: 227-232.

It has become self-evident that the most important geographical factor that directs the people movements is the relief – the geological formation – of the terrain. The natural barriers, such as high mountain ranges, are the determinants that make people movements prohibitive or not. For the main theme of the monograph the migratory itineraries of the I.E. is of utmost importance. They corroborate and validate also the proposed new hypothesis. The natural barriers are shown on Map 6.

Map 6

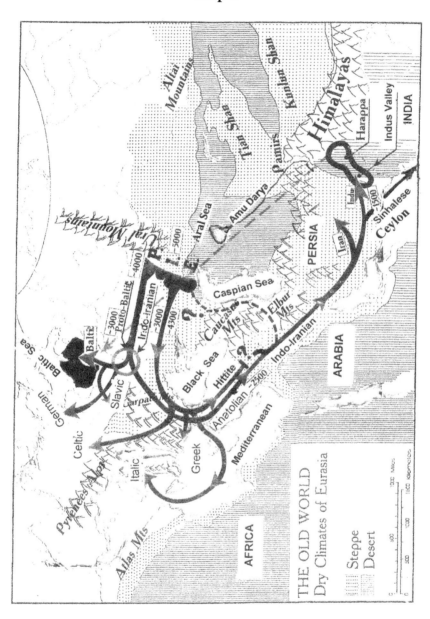

Migratory pathways of the Indo-Iranians, from Europe to India.
Dotted line: ---------- direction (obsolete today) of migration of the
Indo-Germanisch as formulated by German linguists in 19th century.

CHAPTER 6: DISCUSSION AND CONCLUSIONS

The Historical Setting

The French historian Paul Veyne in his book *The Greeks, Have They Believed In Their Myths?* comments on the Greek philosophers of the classic period:

> *"Their solution was to believe in one verity on the things and on the man. The future of the world is one perpetual commencement, since all is destroyed by the periodic catastrophes, and the mythic age is nothing more than the last of these periods."* (Veyne: 133).

Not necessarily having a 'catastrophe', every new idea or new archaeological find can shake and even reverse dominant scientific theories and hypotheses. A prominent example is the archaeological discovery, at the beginning of 20th century, of the ruins of two great ancient cities (Harappa and Mohenjo-Daro) in the Indus River Valley. These two cities formed the core of the Harappan culture, also known as the Civilization of the Indus Valley, which flourished from 3000-1500 BC (Kosambi: 55-56). These archaeological discoveries have proven that the decline of this Civilization, about 1500 BC, coincided with the intrusion of the semi-nomadic Indic people (from the Indo-Iranian branch) coming from the West (from Europe). The discovery has partly reversed the established hypothesis about the Indo-Europeans, held by historians and linguists since the 19th century. Thus the Indo-European question was raised again: how did their languages disperse and what were the itinereries of their migrations?

Near the end of the 20th century a new cladistic Indo-European language tree was developed that surprised the linguistic community. The new scientific findings, concerning the diffusion of I.E. languages, were disclosed by the linguists R. Ringe and Ann Taylor of the

University of Pennsylvania in Philadelphia. With the help of specialist mathematicians and powerful computers they created a new cladistic Indo-European language tree (Figure 1). They found that the Proto-Baltic branch was the last to separate from the Indo-Iranian branch. The second surprise was the finding that the Germanic and Slavic languages have separated from the Proto-Baltic branch. This raises a fundamental question: when and where did the Indo-Iranians separate from the Proto-Baltic branch? An answer to this question is provided by the archaeological discoveries of the 20th century and the new hypothesis presented in the previous pages. It is not surprising that the Germanic and Slavic people formed the common Germano-Slavic-Baltic branch (the Proto-Baltic). Being the first to separate, the Germanic people moved further west, thus encountering the indigenous populations, the Celts and probably also the Italics. Therefore, by the process of transculturation, their language changed the most. The Balto-Slavic group, and in particular the Baltic people, remained close to where they separated from the Proto-Indo-Iranians. The Baltic people were minimally exposed to non-Indo-European speaking peoples, and they continued to use their I.E. language, thus retaining its original structure. Therefore, the Baltic languages are often called archaic by linguists, but without further explanation as to how and where such archaism evolved.

The New Perspective

The Status of the Dainas and the Vedic Hymns

The Vedic hymns of Rg-veda have been composed between 1500-1200 BC, transmitted by memorization since and published in classic Sanscrit in 17th century. They are the oldest written material of the Indo-Europeans. The Latvian mythological Dainas are also transmitted by memorization since the separation, circa 3000 BC, between the Proto-Baltic and Indo-Iranian branches, and published in Latvian at the end of 20th century. These analogous common historical characteristics point to the fact that the ideology contained in Latvian mythological Dainas is older than that of Vedic Sanscrit. After the separation from the Proto-Baltic branch the Indo-Iranian languages, underwent significant changes. During some 1500 years, these changes were the result of contact with non-Indo-European speaking peoples and cultures, encountered along the migratory routes. From the Near East they acquired the art of writing and about 600 BC the first Vedic Sanscrit texts of the Vedic hymns were produced. When the Indic speaking people (branch of Indo-Iranians) entered India they brought with them orally transmitted ancient ideology and beliefs, even though these have been influenced and altered by non-I.E. languages. Regardless of these influences, the Vedic hymns still reflect certain mythological motifs inherited from their I.E. ancestors. (Mallory : 36-37).

The appearance of multiple Gods is an indication that a celestial hierarchy had already been established when the poets conceived their hymns. By glorifying the Gods, these poets reveal their submission to the supreme deities.This is contrary to the language of the Dainas, where Dievs is never glorified, but often sojourns among the people and participates in their daily activities. The structure of the Dainas has retained its original archaic characteristics, similar to the Vedic hymns: the first two lines of the quatrain consist of a statement about the activities of the deities and the last two lines provide an answer on the effects of these activities. The structure of the Vedic hymns is similar as pointed out by Louis Renou:

> *'These hymns consist of groups of contiguous strophes, forming a question and a response with a common phraseology, in a manner of a catechism'.*(Renou: 11)

By settling in the Baltic region, the Baltic people remained close to where they separated from the Indo-Iranians. They were minimally exposed to foreign influences and therefore longer preserved the ancient language and ideology of the Indo-Europeans. When the Indic branch of Indo-Iranians arrived in India they were separated both historically (by 1000 years) and geographically (6000 km) from their original site of separation from the Proto-Baltic branch. For these reasons it can be deduced that the Baltic languages, and the language of the mythological Dainas in particular, have retained more elements of the common I.E. language than has the Indic language after its arrival in India.

Another important aspect is that the creation of the Vedic hymns ceased around 600 BC, whereas the creation of the Dainas was continued. In any case and regardless of the separation, the common mythological motifs between the Vedic hymns and the Latvian Dainas affirm that both belong to and originate from the common Indo-European people and language. In Chapter 4 of the monograph, the comparative analysis of a significant group of Dainas with the Vedic hymns demonstrates the similarity of certain mythological motifs.

Matriarchy and the Danubians

Although the existence of a matriarchy among the Danubians has already been touched on, this section explores the common elements between the Latvian Dainas, the Danubian semiotic language, the Vedic hymns, and the social structure of the Indo-Europeans. Moreover, an inquiry is pursued into whether or not common elements exist that would support the main theme of the monograph – the circulation of rain/water.

Chronology

The intrusion of the I.E.s into the Baltic region is dated circa 2300 BC and into the Danubian basin circa 3500 BC, some 1000 years earlier. Therefore, the matrifocal social structure in the Baltic region was in existence some 1000 years longer and without interruption since the Paleolithic (Latvijas: 19). This social structure is well reflected in the Latvian Dainas, where the essential terrestrial duties are assigned to the feminine deities, such as Māra, the terrestrial genetrix, and Laima, the deity of fate. In the Danubean social structure these functions were represented by the Great Goddess until the Danubian matriarchy was gradually replaced by the patriarchy introduced by the first waves of the Indo-Europeans. The Great Goddess was replaced by the dominant male deities of the Indo-Europeans, but not totally. The feminine elements of diverse forms have left their traces in indo-europeanized Europe, including the Baltic region. The hybridized Indo-Europeans, when leaving the Danubian region, carried with them the feminine elements further east and, perhaps, even to India. Some traces of the image of Mother Earth, the fluvio-terrestrial deity and universal genetrix, are found in a number of Vedic hymns in the Atharva-Veda (Renou: 268).

This raises a number of new questions:

- How did the feminine deities appear in the Vedic hymns in India?
- Is the Mother Earth in Atharva-Veda just a creation of local character?
- Is the conventional view of patriarchy of I.E. an exageration? [21]
- Were the numerous male deities borrowed along the migratory routes?

A review of the Indo-Iranian (I.E.) social structure is required to reconcile the different aspects of these questions. "Daugthers of the Sun" (hymn 24) and the old mythic name of the earth "Aditi" (hymn 61), as a primitive maternal deity (Renou: 269), invoke the feminine aspect. "The daughters of the Sun" are clearly reflected in the Latvian Dainas as "Saules meitas" (in Latvian). What is the significance of these invocations by the Vedic poets?

By returning to the main theme of the monograph, it can be stated that close similarities prevail between the Latvian Dainas, the semiotic images of the Danubean culture, and the Vedic hymns.

The New Hypothesis

The origin of the Proto-Indo-Europeans, later named the Indo-Europeans, was reviewed previously. Their migration through Eastern Europe, the Danubian basin, the Balkans, and arrival in Anatolia is reasonably well documented. It can be safely assumed that the great majority of Indo-Europeans remained in Europe, while the rest continued to move further east. The first to enter Anatolia were the Kurgan people, the last – the Indo-Iranians. Of interest is a recent archaeological discovery of a Celtic settlement in Central Turkey, an indication that Anatolia was penetrated by various I.E. language groups. Indo-European studies have not yet established what happened to them after their sojourn in Anatolia. A rare exeption is the remark by Indian linguist S. Chatterji:

> *"It is the land of the Balts and the Slavs of present day, which was the Uhrheimat of the Indo-Europeans, and the Vedic Aryans (re. Indo-Iranians) went to India ultimately from the Balto-Slav areas".* (Chatterji: 24).

However, by what itinerary the Balto-Slavs arrived in India was not suggested by S.Chatterji.

The new hypothesis proposes that the Indo-Iranians continued to migrate east through Mesopotamia and the coastal areas of Persia to reach the Indus Valley. This is based on the fact that trading routes existed between the Indus Valley, Persia, Mesopotamia, and Anatolia. In the 20th century in Iran, halfway between India and Iraq, archaeological excavations uncovered a trading post with Indus seals and other trade implements. Thus it was established that people movements could have taken place following the ancient trade route along the coastal lands of the Persian Gulf and Arabian Sea. Therefore, the migratory pathway of the Indo-Iranians to India became a well grounded possibility as proposed by the new hypothesis. It re-establishes the close linguistic relationship between them and the Proto-Baltic branch, as well as the close thematic similarities between the Latvian Dainas and the Vedic hymns. It also confirms the possibility that the Latvian Dainas convey an earlier version than the Vedic hymns of their common mytho-poetic language, and explains the archaism assigned to the Baltic languages by historians and linguists.

A Review of the Proposed Themes

Main Theme

Water was chosen as a leitmotif for the research, because it is recognized as a vital fluid, indispensable for all life forms on earth. Water as such, however, can be found in all mythologies around the globe and therefore would not provide appropriate material for a comparative analysis. For these reasons, it was necessary to find attributes and events associated with water other than those that apply directly to water itself. These attributes provided the key words and key phrases for the comparative analysis.

Two important questions were addressed:

– Which mythological deities participated in the circulation of rain/water?
– What means were used by the deities to ensure its circulation?

The studies of these two questions supported the research and provided convincing answers (results). The comparative analysis was successfully used to decipher the symbolic languages of the Latvian Dainas, as well as the corresponding Vedic hymns.

Danubian texts:

The comparative studies of the Latvian Dainas with the semiotic language of Danubians presented particular difficulties. The mythopoetic texts of the lyrical quatrains have yet to be compared with the semiotic texts, such as painted signs and symbols, which have been discovered on feminine statuettes during archaeological excavations. The interpretation of the aquatic motifs of the signs and symbols is taken from *The Language of the Goddess* by M. Gimbutas.

Thematic overview:

When the texts of the Dainas are compared with the texts of the Vedic hymns and those of the semiotic language of the Danubians, it can be summarized that:

> The Dainas, which are anonymous and collectively created, reveal more clearly the process of circulation of rain-water between the celestial deities and Mother Earth;

> The Vedic hymns describe the circulation of rain/water similarly to the Dainas, with the difference that the individual anonymous poets, while following the vestiges of the oral tradition, have ascribed to the hymns a godly and heroic character;

> The semiotic language of Danubians, which is painted on the feminine statuettes, communicate the same messages that are found in the Latvian Dainas and Vedic hymns.

The New Hypothesis

The migratory itineraries as proposed by the New Hypothesis help to explain why similarities are found between the Dainas and the Vedic hymns and why the feminine deities appear in the Atharva-Veda. It shows that people movements are known to follow trade routes. The importance of natural geographic barriers is highlighted, which has been under-rated in the past.

CONCLUSIONS

The Main Theme

The objective of this monograph was to study the significance of the similarities and the parallelism found in the Latvian Dainas and Vedic hymns. Comparative analysis showed that a thematic mythological affinity exists between the Latvian Dainas and Vedic hymns. What means were available to prove that affinity?

The only available texts were the hymns of the Rg-Veda and the Atharva-Veda, composed about 1200 BC in Vedic Sanscrit, and the Latvian Dainas of an archaic origin, but collected and published at the beginning of the 20th century. At the first reading, numerous mytho-poetic verses of the Dainas and Vedic hymns appear to be incomprehensible and even illogical. For example, how is one to understand the following:

"Dear God rode over the grass with a colt of stone; He brought the leaves for the trees, the green clover for the earth".
(Daina, 34067)

or

"They have harnessed the wind as horses to the yoke; The sons of Rudra have changed their sweat into rain".
(Vedic hymn, Mandala V, H 58.v.7)

Supported by the analysis of the formulaic and semantic structures, the meanings of the representative verses were deciphered by the comparative analysis of similar mythological themes found in the Latvian Dainas and in the corresponding Vedic hymns. This approach was confirmed by Calvert Watkins: *"It's in the thematics where we find the doctrine, ideology, and the culture of the Indo-Europeans"* (Watkins: 270).

By following these principles, the study of the main theme of the monograph – the role of the mythological deities of the rain, water, wind, storm, and Earth – provided several answers:

1. The comprehension of the sense of a significant number of Latvian mythological Dainas
2. The comprehension of the sense of the Vedic hymns devoted to the deity Marut and to the deity Earth
3. A confirmation that the underlying substance of the mytho-poetic verses of the Latvian Dainas and Vedic hymns have originated in a common archaic heritage

The Supportive Themes

The purpose of the two supportive themes, the 'Danubian Matriarchy' and 'The New Hypothesis' have been described in detail on the previous pages. The broadened content of these themes were designed to expand the historical and geographical base for the main theme of the monograph. Four new criteria were established:

1. The Latvian and Lithuanian[22] Dainas represent the most archaic mytho-poetic material to contain the world-view, ideology, and culture of the Indo-Europeans.
2. The appearance of feminine deities in the Atharva-Veda leads to the conclusion that the Indo-European social structure was not as patriarchal as previously postulated by socio-historians.
3. The migratory itineraries of the Indo-Europeans, particularly those of the Indo-Iranians, explain the incurred linguistic changes that appeared in the Vedic hymns soon after their arrival in India.
4. The above criteria lead to the fundamental conclusion: the living Baltic languages, and not the dead Vedic Sanskrit language, represent the oldest Indo-European languages in existence.

Post – Scriptum

The conclusions reached in the research of the main theme of the monograph confirmed that fundamental thematic similarities and parallelism exist between the Latvian Dainas and Vedic hymns. The supportive themes validated these results and further explained how these linguistic similarities - and differences - occurred and, at the same time, outlined also the migratory pathways of the Indo-Europeans from Europe to India.

What are the consequences of these findings?

First, it calls for a review and possible revision of the artificially created P.I.E. language some 110 years ago and since then used as a basic reference source by historians and linguists.

Second, the New Hypothesis fills the geographical gap of migratory pathways and explains how the Indo-Iranians migrated from Anatolia to Persia, to the Indus Valley, and to Ceylon; at present, to the author's knowledge, there is no other scientific explanation available.

NOTES

1a. More information on these events can be found in *Senprūsiu Laisves Kovos* by M. Anysas and in *The Baltic Crusade* by W. Urban.

1. *"....the anthropology seems to be progressively detached from religious studies. The amateurs from various provenances have profited by pervading the domain of religious ethnology.* (Lévi- Strauss, 1 : 235).

2. *"....in fact, we propose that the real constitutive units of the myth are not the isolated relations, but the bundles of relations, and that only with the combinations of such bundles, that the constitutive units acquire significative function".* (Lévi- Strauss, 1 : 242).

3. now - The Baltic Sea

4. The Jatvingians inhabited the territory southeast of Lithuania, between the upper reaches of Pripet, Bug, and Nemunas rivers. Gradually they were absorbed by the Western Slavs (predecessors of Poles) and vanished as a nation in the 16th century. A similar fate was experienced by the Galindians who inhabited the lands of the Oka river basin and the Upper Volga territory (Moscow region). They were defeated and assimilated by Eastern Slavs (predecessors of Russians) in the 13th century. These two Baltic nations disappeared from the maps of Europe.

5. *The Baltic Crusade* (the first book on the subject in any language) by W. Urban contains a detailed account, from a somewhat biased western European viewpoint, of the holy wars against the Baltic peoples. These wars by Christian rulers he describes as follows: *"This type of imperialism was not confined to princes; archbishops also sponsored missionaries for motives that were as much secular as religious, and 'episcopal imperialism' was to be an important aspect of the mission to Livonia* (Northern Latvia and Estonia)". (Urban: 25).

6. The 13th century events in Baltic lands are well described in *Senprūsiu Laisves Kovos* (The freedom wars of the old Prussians) by Dr. M. Anysas. Of interest is a passage that pertains to the ethnocide and genocidic practices of European (mostly German) Crusaders. These followed the proclamation of a holy war against "Pruthenorum Gentes" (Old Prussians), a Bull issued by Pope Gregory X in 1272. The Old Prussian armies, after many years of fighting, were defeated and – *"Against the Pogesanians (western tribe), who continued fighting, the Order launched penal expeditions, ravaging the countryside, slaughtering all males and capturing women and children.....In the words of the chronicler - Prussia now rested in peace"*. (Anysas: 313-316).

7. The ancient Baltic name of the Prussian nation has undergone many historic changes. From the papal Bull of 1272 it inherited the name of "Pruthenorum Gentes". After the annexation by Germany it acquired the name of Ostpreussen (engl. East Prussia). The Germans, however, appropriated for themselves the name "Das Preussen" (engl. Prussia) for the region around their capital Berlin. All of East Prussia was germanized and the Prussian (Baltic) language extinguished by the 17th century. After the 2nd World War East Prussia was divided between the Poles and Russians. Since then the land of the Baltic Prussians has disappeared from the map of Europe.

8. Linguistics and Poetics of Latvian Folk Songs, Essays, Vīķis-Freibergs I: 35.

9. *"These songs (Dainas), of which we have only some remnants, and which have endured the centuries of servitude by preserving the purity of expression and noble allure, evoke a mythology which, in its blossoming, could perhaps compete with the brilliance and the poesy of the most beautiful mythologies of the Indo-European peoples"*. (Jonval: 6).

10. M. Harris, while studying Herder, writes: *"Johann Herder, another firm believer in the unity of the human species, anticipated the Boasian argument against ethnocentrism"*. (Harris: 89).

11. Typology and terminology: There is no precise term for the description of Latvian folk-poetry. The various terms used range from simple everyday

folksongs to philosophical verses containing religio-psychic concepts. Folk-poetry describing every-day life in a farming community can be found around the world in most agricultural societies. The same can also be said about folk-poetry associated with nature and social behaviour. Generally, these types of folksongs were termed as 'folkloric material'. A later classification separated the popular folkloric songs from the ancient verses with mythological content. By the beginning of the 20th century, and this applies in particular to the Latvian Dainas, some linguists noticed similarities between the Baltic term 'daina' and those of Sanscrit 'dhēna' and Avestan 'daēnā'. As metioned before, J.G. Herder described the 'dainas' as an archive of the Latvian people, their science, spirituality, and ancient events. A remarkable notion is also found in G. von Bergman's (1807) collection where the term 'folksongs' is replaced by 'Sinngedichte' (engl. 'Mindsongs'). This term could also be translated as 'songs with mental image'. As an example the two Dainas with 'mental image' that were presented in this monograph, and were also chosen by Herder in his publication of 1807, are not yet fully deciphered nor understood.

12. Two large and noteworthy volumes of Latvian folksongs have been published outside Latvia. Both volumes represent the most complete and authoritative material published on their respective subjects. Each of them offers a summary in English. 1. *MĀTE MĀRA (The Mother Goddess Māra)* by sculptor Arvīds Brastiņš, Cleveland, U.S.A., 1967. This publication contains a comprehensive survey and analysis of the functions of the Goddess Māra. The many illustrations and interpretation of individual folksongs enriches the subject matter. 2. *LATVIEŠU GADS, GADSKĀRTA UN GODI (The Ancient Latvian Time System (Calendar), Festivals, and Celebrations)* by Marģers and Māra Grīns, Latvian Institute, Lincoln, U.S.A., 1983. This large-format book of 450 pages contains Latvian folksongs devoted to the entire lifespan of man complete with the music notes as sung at the respective celebrations. An extensive study of the three suns, cosmological, physical, and mythological, was completed and published as the trilogy *Saules Dainas* (Latvian Sun-songs) by Vaira Vīķis-Freibergs, Helios, Montreal, Canada, i988. Another book, created in honour of the sesquicentennial of the birth of Kr. Barons, *Linguistics and Poetics of Latvian Folk Songs*, was edited and assembled from scholars of eight countries by the same

author (V. V-F.) and published by McGill-Queen's Uviversity Press, Kingston and Montreal, Canada, 1989.

13. *"The knowledge about Latvian mythology has come to us by some fragmentary and tendentious material contained in the chronicles by German priests who came to fight paganism, and also by the popular traditions, proverbs, tales, and songs. These songs are the Dainas that were orally transferred from generation to generation to the present, and provide an extremely rich material about the life and beliefs of the ancient Latvians. (Jonval: 5)"*.

14. *"The intrinsic value attributed to a myth comes from the fact that the events, which supposedly take place in a moment of time, also form its permanent structure. This applies simultaneously to the past, the present, and the future"*. (Lévi-Strauss, 1 :239).

15. *"One thing is certain, and that is the success of the oral transmission of the Vedic texts for over four millennia, which occurred before the appearance of writing, a much more recent invention in India. Even today when the help of writing is available, there exist capable narrators who avoid it totally"*. (Filliozat: 18).

16. The root of the term ʿarā-ysʾ in Latvian can be found in most Indo-European speaking peoples, either as cognats or as a result of diachronic changes; ʿara-reʾ in Latin, terre ʿara-bleʾ in French, ʿara-bleʾ land in English. The infinitive form of the verb ʿartʾ in Latvian designates the work (to plough) by the ʿarāysʾ, however, this term has acquired a different meaning and ʿartʾ today denotes everything ʿart-isticʾ.

17. Some examples of morphophonetic changes in Balto-Slavic and Eglish languages:

Latvian	akm-ens	desmit	jaun-s	vald-īt	las-is
Lithuanian	akm-uo	desimt	nauj-as	vald-yti	lāš-is
Russian	kam-eṇ	desjatị	novij	vlad-et	los-ós
English	stone	hundred	young	rule (wield)	sal-mon

18. *"......from the German Sanskritists who took a leading part in establishing the 'Aryan' (or Indo-Germanic, or Indo-European) bases of the culture of the European peoples, they developed an uncritical and a rather emotional idea that the Baltic peoples came from the East – from Asia – and as they thought, from India. It was a semi-sophisticated homage paid to the ancient culture of India with her Vedas and her primeval wisdom, about which many of the Baltic scholars and writers acquired romantic notions from mid-nineteenth-century German Indology,.........*
But modern science – linguistics, and comparative literature as well as comparative religion, and archaeology and sociology – is now establishing it the other way. It is the land of the Balts and the Slavs of the present day which was the "Uhrheimat" of the Indo-Europeans, and the Vedic Aryans went to India ultimately from the Balto-Slav areas". (Chatterji : 23-24).

19. On the question of the origin of the Anatolians, all rigourous studies have shown that they came from the Balkan region. (Sergent : 409).

20. *"The Singhalese is a dialect spoken in western Ceylon, which has been brought to the island by Indian Buddhists before our era, without doubt – from the Goujerat (Bombay) region -- but having evolved in Dravidian milieu, has become aberrant ; the Mahl, spoken in the Maldive islands is close to it (Singhalese)".* (Sergent : 132).

21. *"All linguistic evidence suggests that Proto-Indo-European society was patrilineal in descent and male dominated according to that much-overworked term patriarchal".* (Mallory : 123).

22. American critic, Robert Payne (in his Forword to *The Green Linden, Selected Lithuanian Folk songs,* Voyages Press, New York, 1964) writes :

> *"The dainos of Lithuania are like those snowfields. They seem to be sung from time immemorial, and they are still being sung. They owe their survival to their poetic power, and also to the very nature of the country which gave them birth, a country hemmed in by forests, swamps and seas, outside the main highways of European civilization. They represent a form of poetry as ancient as anything on this*

earth, for they are essentially spells, incantations, offerings to the gods. Though they are simple and immediately comprehensive, they do not belong to the world we know. There is about them something steady and direct like the eyes of animals. These poems to the gods show no fear, nor do they plead for mercy".

The common characteristics with Latvian Dainas are similarly described by Prof. Vaira Vīķis-Freibergs of Université de Montréal some 20 years ago :

"In Latvian Dainas we find the perception of life as observed by generations and programmed in poetic language. They speak in direct and indirect way about the value system of a people and their relationships with nature and society. It is a Latvian tradition to speak about fundamental questions: what is an individual, what are his/hers morals and ethics, how well do they perform a duty, and what do people say about it. The fundamental question treated in the Dainas is associated with an individual's honour and integrity. These are very deep-seated values inherited from our ancestors".

APPENDIX

On the first page two Lithuanian and Latvian mythological Dainas of a common subject matter are presented. On the following pages a nomenclature of the main Vedic gods and Latvian/Lithuanian family and place names are listed side by side for easy comparison.

Lithuanian (Mallory : 83)	English
Mēnuo sauluže vedē,	The Moon leads (home) the Sun,
Pirma pavasarēli.	In the first of Spring.
Sauluže anksti kēlēs,	The Sun rose early,
Mēnužis atsiskyrē.	The Moon left her.
Mēnuo viens vaikštinējo,	The Moon alone wandered,
Aušrine pamylējo.	With the Dawn (M. Star) he fell in love.
Perkūnas didžiai supykes,	Perkūnas very angry,
Ji kardu perdalijo.	With his sword he cut him to pieces.

Latvian (33950,v3.1)	English
1. Pērkons cirta mēnestiņu	Pērkons cut Mēnesis to pieces
2. Ar aso zobentiņu;	With the sharp sword;
3. Kam atņēma Ausekļam,	Because he took away from Auseklis,
4. Saderētu līgaviņu.	His fiancée, his promised one.

33950 (var.Lines 1 and 2)	English
1. Saule cirta mēnestiņu	Saule cut Mēnesis to pieces
2. Ar aso zobentiņu;	With the sharp sword;

Lines 3 and 4 – DITTO –

These Dainas describe cosmogonic events and suggest that their archaism lead to an early Indo-European epoch.

The Gods: A Reflection on Transposition

The universal definition of 'god' becomes nebulous when we search for it in mythological material, more so in mytho-poetics. Some linguists have suggested that the ancient poets had the tendency, by a process known as 'transposition', to create heros from the gods or the opposite – create gods from the heros. Others have proposed that the celestial events were just the fantasies of Vedic poets when describing the atmospheric turbulences or the seismic terrestrial quakes as the work of the great gods. Thus Max Muller has written : *"I had wished to look at the Vedic religion as a nature worship and nothing else"* (Muller : XXVII). The results of the study in this monograph lead to the same conclusion.

The comparatistes, in the European tradition, have always followed the principal effort to establish divine indo-european nomenclature. Without any real success, many books have been published by historio-linguists to find a convincing definition.

> *"The most believable has revealed itself as misleading: in the vedic 'Dyau`, the sky is oriented differently than in the greek 'Zeus' and 'Jupiter' of Rome, and the comparisons prove almost nothing".* (Dumézil I : 11).

A different approach to the comparison of the Indo-European gods is presented in the Appendix. The names of the Vedic deities as they are encountered in Sanscrit are compared with analogous Latvian and Lithuanian personal, river, and place names that are still used in Latvia and Lithuania today. These names are translated or explained in the adjacent column in English.

In Latvian and Lithuanian the consonant 'j' is pronouced like the letter 'y'. In Latvian two declinations – nominative and genitive forms - are shown, for example: nom. `Dievs`, gen. `Dieva`

SANSCRIT/P.I.E.	LATVIAN/LITHUANIAN	ENGLISH
Vedic gods		
Dyaus, Deva-h	Diev-s,-a/Dievas	God
Deva-Pati	Dievs Pats (latvian)	omnipotent God
	dev-a,-as (latvian)	endowment
Rudra	—	—
*reu-, *rū-	rūkt/rūkti	growl
Marut(s)	—	—
	Maruta/Rūta	name feminine
Parjanya	Pērkon-s.-a/Perkūnas	deity of thunder
*perk-, *perku-	pērkon-s,-a/perkūnas	thunder
Indra	—	—
	Indra	name feminine
	Indrāni (latvian)	place name
	Indr-upe (latvian)	name of river
Vrtra	—	—
	vētra/audra	storm
Vāyu	—	—
	vēy-š,-a/vēyas	wind
Mitra	—	—
	mitra/mitrus	humid
Agni	—	—
	uguns/ugnis	fire
Varuna	—	—
	vara/varu	power
Asvin, Asva	Ūsiņ-š,-a (latvian)	deity of horses
Brahma	—	—
brahmān	Bramanis (latvian)	family name
	Ramanis, Prīmanis	family names
rāma	rāma/ramus	calm
*rem-, *ram-	Rāmava/Rāmove	place of meditation
Véda	Vēdas	Veda
*ueid-, *uid-	vest (infin.)/vesti	to lead
	veda (imp.)	led
	vieds (latvian)	wise, sage
vedhās	vedējs/vadas	leader
Sanscrit (1870)	rakstīt (infin.)/rasyti	to write
Sanscreatr (1725)		

Hanscrit	(1667)	
Udān, Danu	—	—
	ūden-s,-s/vauduo	water

The morphological and semantic similarities are striking: one side lists the ancient names of the Vedic gods and the other the names, words, and thematic terms that are found in the living languages in Latvia and Lithuania today. It was shown earlier in the monograph that the Proto-Baltic and the Indo-Iranian l anguages were, before separation, of a common origin. Therefore, we can presume that the first Vedic poets could, by traditional oral transmission, still remember the personal names, words, and metaphoric expressions of the language of their ancestors.

The process of transposition may seem to be audacious, however, by ignoring it we would be denying an important element that could be useful for future historio-linguistic research. A more recent example of this process is how European immigrants carried across the Atlantic Ocean the names of their ancestors, the cities, rivers, and lakes of their birthplaces, and even the names of their gods, kings, and saints.

SELECTED BIBLIOGRAPHY

Abbreviations: JIES – Journal of Indo-European Studies

AABS – Association of Advanced Baltic Studies

Allegro J M: 'The Sacred Mushroom and the Cross', Hodder and Stoughton, London,1970

Anysas M: 'Senprūsiu Laisves Kovos', Chicago, Illinois, 1968.

Barons Kr, and Wissendorff H: 'Latwju Dainas', vol. 1-7, Jelgava-Petrograd, 1894- 1915.

Bergman von G: Erste Sammlung Lettische Sinngedichte in Livonia', Riga, 1807.

Bloomfield M: 'On Vedic dhena, prayer, song', Journal of the American Oriental Society 46 : 303-308, 1926.

Bourdieu P: 'Outline of a Theory of Practice', Cambridge Uni Press, 1977.

Brastiņš A: 'Māte Māra', Māra, Cleveland, 1967.

Campbell, J: 'The Inner Reaches of Outer Space', Harper, N.Y., 1986.

Chatterji S K: 'Balts and Aryan`s', Indian Institute of Advanced Study, Simla, 1968.

Clifford J. and Marcus G.E: 'Writing Culture', U. of C. Press, Berkeley, 1986.

Dumézil G: 1. 'Mythe et épopée', Gallimard, Paris, 1986.
2. 'Mythes et dieux des I.E.', Flammarion, Paris, 1992.

Filliozat P S: 'L'Inde Classique', Paris, 1992.

Finnegan R: 'Oral Traditions and the Verbal Arts', Routhledge, London, 1992.

Geldner K F: 'Der Rig-Veda', Harvard University Press, Cambridge, 1951.

Gimbutas M: 1. 'The Balts'. Praeger, N.Y., 1968.
2. 'Transformation of Myth through Time', Anthology, Harcourt,1990.
3. 'The Language of the Goddess', Harper & Row, San Francisco, 1989.

Greimas A: 'The Green Linden', Selected Lithuanian Folksongs, Voyages Press, New York, 1964.

Grīns M, and Grīns M: 'Latviešu Gads, Gadskārta un Godi', Latvian Institute, Lincoln, 1983.

Hamp E: 'FISH', JIES, 1, 4, 1973.

Harris M: 'The Rise of Anthropological Theory', Harper Collins, N.Y., 1968.

Herder J G: 'Stimmen der Foelker in Liedern', Marburg, 1807.

Jamison S.W, and Witzel M: 'Vedic Hinduism', Harvard, 1992.

Jonval M: 'Les chansons mythologiques lettonnes', Picart, Paris-Riga, 1929.

Kilbourne-Matossian M: 'Vestiges of the Cult of Mother Goddess in Baltic Folklore' AABS, Columbus, 1973.

Kortlandt F: 'The spread of the Indo-Europeans', JIES, 18, 1-2, 1990.

Kosambi D D: 'Ancient India : A History of its Culture and Civilization', World Publishing, Cleveland, 1969.

Kuiper F B J: 'Ancient Indian Cosmogony', Delhi, 1983.

Kursīte J: 'Latviešu folklora mītu spogulī', Zinātne, Rīga, 1996.

'Latvijas PSR Archeoloģija', Zinātne, Rīga, 1974.

Lévi-Strauss C: `Anthropologie structurale` 1 et 2 ,Plon, Paris, 1957.

Lucy J A: `Whorf's View of the Linguistic Mediation of Thought', Academic Prep. Orlando, 1985.

Malik S C: `Indian Civilization, the Formative Period', Indian Institute of Advanced Study, Simla, 1968.

Mallory J P: `In Search of the Indo-Europeans', Thames & Hudson, London, 1996.

Muller Max: `Vedic Hymns, Oxford, 1891

Oliphant S G: `Sanskrit dhena—Avestan daena—Lithuanian daina, Journal of the American Oriental Society 32: 393-413, 1912.

Paliepa J R: 'Latvju Dainas un Vedu hymnas', Elpa 2, Rīga, Latvia, 2004

Rawlinson G: `Herodotus Histories, Book Club, N.Y., 1997.

Renou L: `Hymnes spéculatives du Veda', Gallimard/UNESCO, Paris, 1956.

Ringe D, and Taylor A: 'The Descent of Germanic Tongues: A New Family Tree', New York Times Service, 1995.

Sergent B: 'Les Indo-Européens', Payot et Rivages, Paris 1995.

Seymour-Smith C: 'Macmillan Dictionary of Anthropology', London, Macmillan Press, 1986.

Tacitus: 'The Agricola and Germania', Penguin, London, 1970.

Trask R L: 'Historical linguistics', Arnold, London, 1996.

Urban W: 'The Baltic Crusade', N. Illinois University Press, DeKalb, Illinois, 1975.

Vernant J P: 'Mythe et pensée chez les Grecs', Maspero, Paris, 1974.

Veyne P: 'Les Grecs ont-ils cru à leurs myths?', Éditions du Seuil, Paris, 1983.

Vīķis-Freibergs V: 1. 'Linguistics and Poetics of Latvian Folk Songs', McGill-Queens, Essays, 1989.
2. 'Myth and Metaphor in Latvian Dainas', AABS, Columbus,1973.

Watkins C: 'Studies in Memory of Warren Cowgill', edited by C. Watkins, Walter de Gruyter, New York, 1987.

Wolf E: 'Europe and the People Without History', Uni. Of California, 1982.

Selected Etymological Dictionaries

Buck C D: 'A Dictionary of Selected Synonyms in the Principal Indo-European Languages', The University of Chicago Press, 1965.

Karulis K: 'Latviešu etimoloģijas vārdnīca', 2 vol., Avots, Rīga, 1992.

Parrinder G, general editor: 'Man and his Gods'-encyclopedia of the worlds religions
Hamlyn, London, 1971

Pokorny J: 'Indogermanisches Etymologisches Worterbuch', Bern, 1959.

Renou L: 'Anthologie Sanscrite', Payot, Paris, 1964.

Reese W L: 'Dictionary of Philosophy and Religion: Eastern and Western Thought', New Jersey, Humanities Press, 1980

Seymur-Smith C: 'Macmillan Dictionary of Anthropology', Macmillan Press, London, 1986
        Montreal, 2009.

CPSIA information can be obtained
at www.ICGtesting.com
Printed in the USA
LVOW03s2333171017
552831LV00002B/251/P